oxygen

Deep Breathing
for the Soul

keri wyatt kent

Revell
Grand Rapids, Michigan

Published by Fleming H. Revell
a division of Baker Publishing Group
P.O. Box 6287, Grand Rapids, MI 49516-6287
www.revellbooks.com

Printed in the United States of America

Library of Congress Cataloging-in-Publication Data
Kent, Keri Wyatt, 1963–
    Oxygen : deep breathing for the soul / Keri Wyatt Kent.
        p.   cm.
    Includes bibliographical references.
    ISBN 10: 0-8007-3068-2 (pbk.)
    ISBN 978-0-8007-3068-0 (pbk.)
    1. Christian women—Prayer-books and devotions—English. 2. Christian women—Religious life. I. Title.
BV4844.K46 2007
242'.643—dc22   2006031254

Published in association with the literary agency of Alive Communications, Inc., 7680 Goddard Street, Suite 200, Colorado Springs, CO 80920.

oxygen

Contents

Contents

Acknowledgments

Books are never conceived or incubated in a vacuum. My sincere thanks to a number of people who helped bring this project to life:

Beth Lagerborg, media manager at MOPS International, who was willing to take a risk and let me write a book that defied categories.

My editor at Revell, Jennifer Leep, who lives out her love for the Lord, and believes in my work and in me in a way that makes me feel pure gratitude. What a blessing it is to work with you!

My friend and fellow writer, Diane Markins, who offered me a quiet space in the desert where God dared me to write this book.

The faithful small group in Irvine, California, who've read all my books and affirmed God's plan for this book: Cathy Erickson, Lynne Yadlin, Lavender Florance, Carol Sartain, Kelly Hill, Jenny Feliciano, Jenny Jack, Michelle McCoy, and Debbie Hotchkiss.

Most importantly, thank you to my sweet family: Scot, Melanie, and Aaron. Thanks for your love, support, suggestions, and reminding me to just breathe!

Introduction

It's 8:00 a.m., and I just got off the phone with my friend Jo. The details of car pools and playdates (our kids are good friends too), the little frustrations of getting our families out the door this morning, the fluff and substance of life swirl through our conversation. We laugh, we listen, we just check in—it's something we do every day or two. Nothing is forced; we talk easily and lightly. She wonders if I will join her at exercise class this morning, but I tell her I've got to write. After giving me a bit of good-natured grief about not working out, she asks me about my writing project and really listens.

It helps me as a mom and as a person to have a friend or two I can connect with to laugh about the crazy things our families do, to encourage, and to be encouraged by. Someone who will listen and who I'm glad to listen to. I'm blessed to have Jo and a few other close friends in my life.

When we feel like life is overwhelming and busy, sometimes we just need to slow down and breathe. To create some space. But space for what? Space for a connection—with a friend. If you're blessed to have a friend like mine, be grateful. And be gracious—don't burden that friend to meet all your needs, because that is simply not going to happen. One person cannot do it. Yet our souls long to be heard, to connect. That's a legitimate desire. To fulfill it, we must create space not just for other people but for someone greater than ourselves.

Usually this conversation is quieter—sometimes when I talk with Jesus, it looks like I'm just sitting and looking out the window. I try to be still, to breathe deeply and slowly just for a few minutes. But at other times it's more similar to my phone conversation with Jo—I'll talk to Jesus about my complaints about my kids or husband, excitement about a new project, or frustration with my sometimes ragged and overwhelmed self. Since I can't call Jesus on the phone, I use some other simple ways to connect with him. I can talk to him, I can listen, I can spend time with him—even if it's only a few minutes. If you're wondering how you might possibly do that, this book is for you.

Jesus said, "Walk with me and work with me—watch how I do it. Learn the unforced rhythms of grace. I won't lay anything heavy or ill-fitting on you. Keep company with me and you'll learn to live freely and lightly" (Matt. 11:28–29 Message).

Through the practices in this book, you can develop a friendship with Jesus that will help you to breathe deeper, to live freely and lightly. To walk in the unforced rhythms of grace.

When he was here on earth, Jesus said a lot of interesting things. Some of us have heard them so often that frankly, they may seem a bit stale. But at the time, Jesus was really fresh.

The people Jesus talked to and taught—that is, first-century Jews—had a word for this. They said he had *shmikah*. Our version of the Bible sometimes translates this as "authority." For example, when it says, "The crowds were amazed at his teaching, because he taught as one who had authority, and not as their teachers of the law" (Matt. 7:28–29).

Jesus was a breath of fresh air. He didn't offer something others had offered before but a new kind of life, a new interpretation of how to live God's way.[1]

Jesus's Fresh Ideas

I think Jesus is still fresh, still offering not tired religion but an amazing relationship. His ideas hover toward the radical: loving your enemies, serving others instead of trying to get ahead, that kind of thing. I mean, do we actually do these things, even if we say we have Christian faith? Jesus continues to offer us a way to live that will bring us joy and freedom.

Check out the kind of things he said (as recorded by one of his closest friends, John):

> You will know the truth, and the truth will set you free.
>
> *John 8:32*

Later he said he was, among other things, "the truth" (John 14:6). So knowing him, knowing the truth, sets us free. This was radically different from anything anyone else was teaching at the time—or has taught since.

> A new command I give you: Love one another. As I have loved you, so you must love one another.
>
> *John 13:34*

Here's that newness, authority, *shmikah* again. The Jews lived by the Torah, the law (we still have the Torah today—it's the first five books of the Old Testament of the Bible). The people of Jesus's day focused on living by God's law—which was, and in fact still is, a good way to live. But Jesus says God's way can be summed up by one thing: just love. He was giving a new command, although it fulfilled the old commands. Jesus said, to live out God's law, just love God and love others. It's how to live.

He promised his followers (including you and me, should we choose to follow him):

> My peace I give you. I do not give to you as the world gives.
>
> *John 14:27*

> I have told you this so that my joy may be in you and that your joy may be complete.
>
> *John 15:11*

Jesus usually made comments like this after telling his disciples really depressing things, like the fact that people would hate them and persecute them or that he was going to die. I told you he was a little, well, *different*. But then he'd say, "Don't be afraid, because you can have my peace, my joy. And it obviously does not depend on your circumstances."

He also said:

> I have come that they may have life, and have it to the full.
>
> *John 10:10*

A full life. What does that mean? Some scholars translate the word *full* in these verses as "complete" or "abundant."

You may feel that your life is very full. As in crowded. Busy. Stuffed. And yet something is missing. Sometimes it doesn't feel complete at all.

You're doing a lot, caring for a lot of people—doing the parenting thing, trying to love and support your spouse, maybe providing some kind of care to your parents or in-laws as they get older. You take care of things at work, perhaps. Life is full, even too full. But maybe it's not as fulfilling as you would like, which seems ironic.

Jesus, true to form, meant something completely different when he talked about life to the full. He meant an abundant life. A satisfying life. A fulfilling life. One that filled you up with those other things he talked about: love, joy, peace, freedom.

Sounds good, doesn't it? Wouldn't it be great if right now—not someday when your kids get older or you get a better job or your husband somehow transforms into Mr. Wonderful, but *now*—you could have this kind of abundantly loving, peaceful, joyful life?

How do we get there? From a life that feels just stuffed with too much responsibility and pressure to a life that feels abundant and full? To a life that's complete? To this life Jesus promised us?

Well, look at those verses again. Jesus said things like "*I've* come," "*I* give," "*my* peace," and "*my* joy." We can't create this stuff for ourselves. He's the one who's got what we want. So it seems to me that the best way to get this kind of full life, this freedom and abundance of joy, peace, and love, is to hang with Jesus.

But he's not here, not in the flesh, anyway. He's here spiritually, for sure, but sometimes that's hard to get your mind around. Especially when you are busy, worried, and distracted. It is possible to experience Jesus's presence, though. You've got to slow down a bit. And begin to pay attention.

Spending Time with Jesus

The Bible offers us a chance to hang around with Jesus. To read a story about him and reflect on it deeply enough that it feels like we're really with him, which, in a way, we are.

That's what this book is about: finding ways to simply spend time with Jesus. Ways to spend time with him so that we can let him give us that life that he talked about: life to the full, life abundantly. To breathe in his presence in a deep and meaningful way. To slow down, just a few minutes at a time, to notice what Jesus is like and what he has to say.

Maybe you've known Jesus for a while, and you're thinking, "I've been trying to get that abundant life. I keep going to Bible study and volunteering for everything and serving my family and everyone else till I'm exhausted. And frankly, that's not really working very well for me anymore."

Or maybe you used to have this great friendship with Jesus. And then you had kids, or got a new job, or both. Or you moved and can't find a church, or your marriage hit a rough patch and you're distracted by that. So now the memories of that spiritual relationship, of mornings when you had time to yourself to read or pray, they're like a hazy dream. And you think, "My life is so full of other stuff that I can't fit Jesus in." You're a little afraid. You think, "He must be so mad at me because I just cannot find the energy or the time to relate to him in the way that used to seem so meaningful to me."

But Jesus knows you. And he says, "Ask and you will receive, and your joy will be complete" (John 16:24). The King James Version says, "that your joy may be full."

Wouldn't it be great if you could find a new way of life? A way of love, peace, and joy—in abundance? That's what Jesus offered to the people he walked around with on this planet two thousand years ago, and that's what he is offering to you. A breath of fresh air. An abundant life. Really! And that's what this book is offering you: a new way of relating to Jesus that is based on some very old ways.

This book is a guide to some ways to practice your faith that will allow you to simply breathe in God's presence. I hate to call them methods; that sounds so contrived. They are just ways of being with God and his Word, and they've been part of Christian tradition and practice for centuries. They are ways we can learn to be contemplative, to pay attention. They're starting to become popular again because, frankly, they work really well. They take us into an authentic encounter with God, if we make the focus God rather than the practice itself.

Each of the Bible's original languages (Greek and Hebrew) has a word that can be translated both "breath" and "spirit." This is not just a coincidence. God's Spirit is as close as the air we breathe. The language expresses a reality and a desire: God is everywhere, all around us, like the air. We need him not just around us but *in* us, like oxygen. The Spirit's presence is life-giving, life-essential. All of us, deep within, have a longing for that presence.

Often we run through life breathing shallowly. Health experts say we can improve our physical health by simply taking time to do deep breathing. I think the same is true of our spiritual life.

This book provides practices to teach you to do the spiritual equivalent of deep breathing exercises. My prayer is that it will help you to tune in to that still, small voice, to welcome Christ into your everyday experience and into your very being. To listen to what God is saying. To help you create some space to meet with God, to visit with Jesus.

How to Use This Book

This is not a high-pressure, intense study. Instead of a verse or passage for each day, there's a scene from the life of Jesus every week. That's right, one Scripture passage for the week. You're going to reflect on it through your week in various ways, using some practices that will help you breathe more deeply, spiritually speaking. You're going to slow down and breathe the Bible in, letting it become a part of you and nourish you the way air does when you inhale.

This book is not a traditional devotional or Bible study—but it is designed to guide you as you read the Bible and pray. It's a tool to help you in your devotional life. You don't have to "do" this book every day. Each week has three exercises plus a Sabbath exercise, so you can use it every other day. Or you can use it in another way that fits your life. If you have very small children, you probably struggle to have a daily time with God. When my kids were toddlers, I felt like leisurely daily devotions went the way of long, romantic dinners with my spouse and showering before noon. If you have a demanding job, you may wrestle with distractions when you do get a chance to pray. When I was working full-time as a newspaper reporter, I'd sit down to pray and end up writing a work to-do list in my journal.

Whatever your situation, this book is not another obligation to stuff into your busy life. It's a guide, a tool to move you toward a deeper relationship with Jesus.

Each week you'll read just one Scripture passage and reflect on it by trying different spiritual practices. You'll learn about these practices by doing them. While they are labeled for day one, day two, and day three, you can do them at any time, in any order.

You can skip one, or if you really like a certain exercise, feel free to do it more than once.

I've included the Scripture text for you each week, to make the book easier to use. Mostly I quote from Today's New International Version, but some weeks I use The Message or The New Living Translation. But I recommend that at least once each week, you pull out your own Bible and read the passage from there. It's a good practice to look things up. Just looking at a passage in the Bible reminds us that each of these stories has a larger context in the life of Jesus, and beyond that, in the history of God's people. If you don't have a Bible, get one, or go to www.biblegateway.com, where you can read any passage of almost any version with the click of a mouse.

To optimize this book, get some index cards. Go for brightly colored ones or small ones you can clip on a ring. Find some that reflect your personality—don't just get plain white ones, unless you want to embellish them with stickers or some other artsy touch. Throughout this book, you'll be directed to write just a sentence or two on an index card. I recommend using one card per week. Carry the card, your "life card," with you all the time. Jesus promised us abundant life, and this card will remind you what that looks like. While you may not use the book daily, I recommend using the card almost constantly.

Keep your life card with you in your purse, pocket, briefcase, diaper bag, whatever. When you get a moment (while riding the train to work, waiting at the pediatrician's office, feeding the baby, brushing your teeth before bed), look at the card. Take a few slow, deep breaths, both physically and spiritually. Or tape the card above the sink so you can read it while doing the dishes or other chores and remember how God spoke to you through his Word. It will be like an oxygen mask for your soul.

You know the drill when you get on an airplane—they give you instructions about what to do in an emergency. "Oxygen masks will drop from the ceiling if needed," the smiling flight attendant on the video says. Then she reminds you, "If you are

What about My Kids?

traveling with small children, put your own mask on first. Then assist those around you."

Why? Because if you try to help other people put their masks on first, you're going to pass out before you can help them. Then you will all be in trouble. Not taking care of yourself first will hurt those you are trying to help. You need some air if you are going to be any good to anyone else.

Look at Deuteronomy 6:6–7. It says first that God's commands are "to be upon your heart" (v. 6 NIV). To get something upon your heart, you have to meditate on it, or think about it, yourself. Only after that happens, only after you have let God's love permeate your life and your heart, can you move on to the next thing, which is to "impress them on your children" (v. 7 NIV). Put on your own oxygen mask first.

If you are traveling through life these days with small children—your own or even nieces or nephews or friends' kids—are you putting on your own oxygen mask first? Are you taking care of yourself, of your own soul, first? Don't confuse survival with selfishness—it is not selfish to take care of yourself. Does your soul have any fresh air, any room to breathe? Or are you flailing around, gasping for air, trying really, really hard to do things for other people that you

If you are a parent, you probably want to help your children get to know Jesus better too. You not only want an abundant life for yourself, you'd like to invite your kids into that kind of life. I mean, that's what God tells us we should do. The Bible says, **"These commandments that I give you today are to be upon your hearts. Impress them upon your children. Talk about them when you sit at home and when you walk along the road, when you lie down and when you get up"** (Deut. 6:6–7 NIV). So you want to find a way to do that—to disciple your kids or at least get them talking about their faith. But you're not sure how.

Sometimes as parents we worry more about our kids than about ourselves. We care for them first and ourselves last, if at all. But you can't give your kids something you don't have yourself. This book will offer you a chance to learn some things. Then you will find some suggestions about how to share some of what you are learning with your kids in a relaxed way, to teach them what God is teaching you, if you want to. But you know what? Sometimes you just need to take care of yourself. Ease up on caring for everyone else. The sharing it with your kids part is completely optional. It's not required. So relax, okay?

17

don't seem to have the power to do? Probably so. Maybe it's why you picked up this book.

This book is fresh air for your soul so that you can breathe. So that you can assist those around you and have enough oxygen to keep you strong and able. It's not your own power that enables you to do this. It's the fresh, abundant air that flows through the mask that keeps you strong, that moves you toward freedom.

Freedom

If you are caring for small kids or an aging parent, if your work seems to consume all of your time, or if your life is just too crowded, you may feel like you simply cannot connect with God every day. But you can. Maybe not the way you think you are supposed to or the way you used to. But that's okay. Jesus is making all things new. This book will help you connect on a daily basis by freeing you from the obligation of the traditional "quiet time."

I suggest that you aim for a weekly appointment with God. If you have kids, get a sitter, your spouse, or a friend to watch them, and get out of the house—away from the phone and the guilt-triggering undone housework. Or take one lunch hour a week to be alone. Take this book with you. Go to a library, coffee shop, or park. Read the week's Scripture and try one or two of the practices. Experiment. Most of all, take your time. This is not a time to accomplish but rather to simply be with God in an unhurried way. Ask God to guide you into a life that is full and abundant, rather than just crazy busy.

On days you can't get away or find even a moment to pray, relax. Know that Jesus is still nearby. Connect for even just two minutes by reading over what you've jotted on that index card, your life card. Spend a few minutes asking for his help and guidance just before you get out of bed. Choose not to argue with your husband, even when you are right. Choose to be kind when your boss is being a jerk. Or make this your spiritual practice for the day: simply sing "Jesus Loves Me" to your kids, looking into their eyes and really believing it. These things are enough—enough air to breathe, enough to pique your desire for deeper breathing.

If your kids are a little older or you don't have children, it may be easier for you to use this book daily or every couple of days. Do what works for you. Just don't start feeling smug about using it every day, if that's what you do. Stick with the one passage per week; just try some other practices related to it. Or you may want to alternate the more contemplative practices in this book with a more academic, study-oriented book. It's up to you. The goal here is freedom and abundant life. Not rule-keeping or achieving. You'll notice this book didn't come with any schedules or dates or a set of gold stars.

Each week will end with a Sabbath Reflection, which is a short essay on one aspect of the week's Scripture, along with discussion questions that you can do by yourself or with your family or others. Keeping a Sabbath is another practice I believe is essential if we are to have the joy, peace, and fullness of life that Jesus offers. We must stop, we must rest, sometime in our week. Again, it's not to keep the rules but rather to take a deep breath, to keep ourselves sane and alive—alive to the full.

My earlier book, *Breathe*, has several chapters on Sabbath-keeping that will give you some practical help in incorporating this practice into your family life. In this book, each week's Sabbath Reflection will guide you toward making this a part of your life.[2]

If you are not used to keeping a Sabbath, you may want to start with simply having a Sabbath meal. Sabbath traditionally begins at sunset, so you may want to have a family meal on Saturday evening.

During that meal read the Scripture that, hopefully, you have been reading and thinking about throughout the week. Then read the Sabbath Reflection. You may want to discuss the ideas in it with the people you live with or with friends, if that works for you. You may want to make this something that is just for you. And that is okay. If you decide to share it with others, keep things relaxed. This is not school; it's a conversation. If you have children, you may want to adapt the reflection and add your own thoughts to fit your kids' attention spans and ages. When your kids share something, don't correct them. Say, "Tell me more about that." And then listen.

Don't try to force small children to sit still to participate in this conversation. Let them simply listen to the conversation, to participate as much or as little as they want. Let toddlers move around the room or sit on your lap if they want to. You can let little ones draw pictures to illustrate the Bible story. Don't force it or feel obligated, though. Pay attention to what you need.

Be open to opportunities to share what you are learning with others throughout your week. But don't feel like you have to. And don't even *think* about trying to "do devotions" with your kids if you haven't taken time to do at least one of the exercises *by yourself*. You cannot guide anyone else into something that you are not experiencing. You need to put on your own oxygen mask first!

The Practices

In addition to helping you in Sabbath-keeping, this book will guide you into experiencing six other spiritual practices, three each week. Here's an overview of the six practices—what they are and a bit of background about each one. If you find that you love certain practices and they really help you to connect with God, use them more often.

Deep listening: Since about AD 500, Christians have been using this practice as a way to pray and listen to Scripture. Read slowly, letting the words sink into your soul, listening for the one word or phrase that touches you most deeply. The monk who came up with this method, Saint Benedict, called it *lectio divina*, which is Latin for "divine word" or "sacred reading." And that is what it is—a word from God. It's a way to meditate on Scripture by listening for God's word to you and then responding to that word. It's breathing in God's Word, breathing out a prayer. You read a passage several times, spending time in silence between readings.

Traditionally this practice includes four parts: reading, meditation, prayer, and contemplation. Each time we do this practice, I'll more or less guide you through these steps.[3]

Deep listening to Scripture requires us to be open to what God is saying. It is *formational* reading—that is, reading that forms us, rather than simply *informs* us. As Robert Mulholland explains, "In informational reading, we seek to grasp the control, to master the text. . . . in formational reading . . . allow the text to master you. In reading the Bible, this means we come to the text with an openness to hear, to receive, to respond, to be a servant of the Word rather than a master of the text. Such openness requires an abandonment of the false self and its habitual temptation to control the text for its own purposes."[4]

Journaling: You may think, "I'm not a writer" or "I'm a terrible speller." Let go of that negative self-talk. Your journal is not for others to see or critique. And it's not for you to critique, for that matter. Get a blank book and some nice colored pens. Don't write with just plain old black or blue ink—you're not filling out a tax form, you're exploring your soul. If you'd rather journal on your life card, with a single sentence at a time, that is fine. If you want to draw or sketch, great. This book is about freedom, not rules. Don't worry; I'll guide you through the process. Because our physical body is involved in the process of writing, it opens up new thoughts, and it keeps us on track mentally. You don't have to write perfect sentences—make lists if you want. Misspell things on purpose if you want. If you are worried someone will read it, get one of those little-girl diaries with a lock and hide it in your underwear drawer. Really. But do try journaling.

Being there: Have you ever read a biography or a great novel and felt so swept up in the story that the characters in the book became real to you? Reading their story, you felt like you were there, spending time with them. You felt like you got to know them, so much so that you may have missed them once you finished the book.

What I call the "being there" practice has traditionally been called Gospel meditation or the Ignatian method. Another monk (those monks are just full of great ideas, aren't they?), Saint Ignatius of Loyola, instructed his followers to spend time with Jesus by imagining themselves in the Gospel story. This is simply another way to reflect or meditate on the Bible, a way of praying by listening to Jesus. It is a way of being there, in the story, with him. As one website puts it, "Think of the Ignatian Method—named after Ignatius of Loyola (1491–1556)—as a sort of virtual experience of the scripture where you read the scripture and then create in your mind a short film about what you read."[5]

Dr. David Benner writes, "Gospel meditation provides an opportunity to enter specific moments in Jesus' life and thereby share his experience. Shared experience is the core of any friendship. And Spirit-guided meditation on the life of Jesus provides this possibility."[6]

Breath prayer: A breath prayer is a short prayer that can be prayed in the space of one breath. It expresses our love for God and our desire for God's touch in our lives. Usually a breath prayer combines a name for God (or Jesus or the Spirit) with a deep desire of our souls, forming a single sentence that we can pray. It can be an intercession or simply a meditation on God. Sometimes it is a form of confession or self-examination. A classic breath prayer, used for centuries, comes from Luke 18:13: "Lord Jesus Christ, have mercy on me, a sinner."

A breath prayer is a way of focusing our minds on or meditating on Jesus, letting go of distractions so that we can simply be with him in his presence. We breathe in his name, his presence; we exhale and release our need to his care. Psalm 1:2 exhorts us to meditate on God's Word, to delight in it. Unlike Eastern meditation practices, which focus on emptying the mind completely, a breath prayer is a way of filling our mind—but filling it with God alone and nothing else. It is like sitting in companionable silence with God, not having to talk but being aware of his company, his loving and accepting presence.

Solitude: Solitude is simply being alone with God. Simple as it may sound, it's not an easy thing to practice. Solitude and silence are companions, and while we can experience them separately (we can be silent in a crowd, or alone but not quiet), they enhance one another. We live in a noisy world where people demand our time and clamor for our words and our actions. When we carve out time to be alone, we get a chance to really breathe in God's presence, especially if we can eliminate noise and distractions. We get a chance to rest, even from our own words. Most importantly, in solitude we embrace silence. We obey God's command, "Be still, and know that I am God" (Ps. 46:10). God is God, and we are not.

Again, this is hard for people like us, who are conditioned to need noise almost constantly, who equate activity with self-worth. But the rewards of spending time in solitude are great. If we let it, solitude can create in us an inner calm, a steady awareness that God is as close as the air we breathe. When we spend time alone with God, it is easier to carry him in our hearts and minds when we are with other people.

Kindness: Jesus said over and over that the key to spiritual life is to love God and love other people. And you really can't do one and not the other, not authentically, anyway. The Bible tells us we should love not just with words but "with actions and in truth" (1 John 3:18).[7] This practice will ask you to put some feet to your faith, to remember that your life is not just about you or even about just you and God. It's about loving others, about accomplishing God's purposes. This practice will sometimes ask you to pray for someone other than yourself. Pray for friends and family who are struggling. Ask God to bring to mind people to pray for. Listen to what God is telling you about their needs, and then do something about it. Meet those needs with some small kindnesses. Step out of your comfort zone once in a while, and you'll find that when you step out to love others, you'll experience God in a deeper, fresh way.

These practices are designed to help you focus on the Scripture of the week, to go a little deeper. Staying with one passage per week may make you feel impatient, but stick with it. What's the hurry? By slowing down and looking at the same passage for several days, you can allow it to really soak in. To absorb the passage, make it a part of yourself.

My prayer for you as you use this book is that you will truly breathe in Jesus's presence, get to know him in a deeper way, experience the peace and joy of intimate relationship with him, and know that he really is as close as the air you breathe. I pray that you would have life and have it to the full.

Week One Matthew 7:1–8

Don't Judge—Ask, Seek, Knock

"Do not judge, or you too will be judged. For in the same way you judge others, you will be judged, and with the measure you use, it will be measured to you.

"Why do you look at the speck of sawdust in someone else's eye and pay no attention to the plank in your own eye? How can you say, 'Let me take the speck out of your eye,' when all the time there is a plank in your own eye? You hypocrite, first take the plank out of your own eye, and then you will see clearly to remove the speck from the other person's eye.

"Do not give dogs what is sacred; do not throw your pearls to pigs. If you do, they may trample them under their feet, and then turn and tear you to pieces.

"Ask and it will be given to you; seek and you will find; knock and the door will be opened to you. For everyone who asks receives; those who seek find; and to those who knock, the door will be opened."

Matthew 7:1–8

Day One: Deep Listening

In this practice, remember, you are listening to God through his Word, the Bible. Deep listening is a method of both meditating on Scripture and praying, of hearing and then responding.

Take a few moments to settle yourself. Take a deep breath, and release any tension in your body. Ask God to simply meet you and speak to you through this passage. Especially with this particular passage, remember that he does not condemn you. Listen for the voice of love. If you hear the voice of shame, that is not God's voice.

Read through the passage slowly, out loud if possible. Listen for the word or phrase that stands out to you. After you read, spend several minutes in silence. Let the word that stood out echo in your mind.

As you read, stay open and trusting, knowing that even Jesus's words of instruction are given to you bathed in his love.

Read slowly through the passage again, listening for the word, phrase, or thought that seems to resonate with you. Spend some time simply turning that word or phrase over in your mind. What does God want to say to you? Is there some encouragement or challenge from him in this word? What does he want you to know?

Spend as long as you need in silence, thinking about what God has said. When you are ready, read the passage one more time, listening again for God's word to you. Remember that he speaks with the voice of love. Is there something he wants you to do? Is he inviting you into a deeper intimacy with him? Is he asking you to go deeper in your seeking of him and his will? Reflect on what he's said to you. Let this time lead you into a dialogue with God or a comfortable silence.

End your time by thanking him for speaking with you through his Word. Write a sentence or two on your life card about what God has said to you.

Day Two: Journaling

This week's passage can easily be divided into two sections: verses 1–6 and verses 7–12. You may choose to focus on one or the other, as the Spirit leads. If you prefer, do this exercise twice, looking at one section one day, the second on another day.

If you choose to focus on verses 1–6, journal about the following questions:

Think of someone who lives in a way you disapprove of. Perhaps it is a family member (say, a sibling) or a friend who has hurt you. How have you judged this person? What is the "speck" in their eye? Go ahead and name it. (It may feel to you like more than a speck.)

Now spend some time just brainstorming on paper about possible specks or planks that might be in your own eye—faults that you might possibly (we're not saying definitely) have in your own life. If you cannot think of any, think about your attitude toward the person you just wrote about. Ask God to gently show you the plank in your own eye.

Judging is wrong, but allowing people to mistreat you is not the alternative, as Jesus points out in verse 6. You can love someone but still not allow them to hurt you. Journal about how you might set boundaries with the person in question—not judging them, but not allowing them to mistreat you either. Do you need to distance yourself physically or emotionally from someone?

If you feel God is leading you to focus on verses 7–12, journal about the following questions:

Jesus tells us to ask, to seek, and to knock. What are you asking Jesus for? What are you seeking? Let the words flow on paper—what is your deep desire?

Do you believe that your heavenly Father will give you good gifts? What are some of the gifts that he's already given you? What are you grateful for?

Write a prayer based on your desire and gratitude.

Pick one thought from your journaling experience and copy it onto your life card.

Day Three: Breath Prayer

Read through the passage again. Look at your life card and your journal. Do you notice a theme? What desires have arisen from your encounter with this passage of Scripture?

What name for God or what aspect of his character have you been aware of through your meditations this week? Perhaps you've seen him as "Generous Father" or "Compassionate Judge." Or maybe you've become aware of your need for forgiveness because you have judged others or because you have not sought after God with your whole heart.

Combine whatever name for God has become meaningful for you this week with that deep desire into a short one-sentence prayer.

Spend some time just sitting, listening to God, breathing slowly and deeply. Use your breath prayer to focus your attention: God's name on the inhale, your need on the exhale.

Write the prayer on your life card and carry it with you this week. Use the breath prayer any time you have a moment to connect with God.

Sabbath Reflection

Read the text out loud. Then read slowly through this reflection. It's up to you whether to include your family or others in this practice. If you do include children, depending on their ages, you can read this to them, summarize it, or simply ask them for their observations about the story. If you have a children's Bible, you could read the story from that version. Be open to the idea that others may have some insights that God can use to speak to you. You can use the questions at the end with others or on your own. Use as many or as few of the questions as you like.

What does it mean to ask, to seek, to knock? Jesus says to his followers, "Everyone who asks receives" (Matt. 7:8). Asks what? Perhaps more importantly, receives what?

An elder at my church once told me about a woman who came to a monthly prayer meeting asking for prayer to be healed of a chronic illness. The illness never went away. But the woman's heart was healed. God changed her attitude as she continued to ask God for help. She went from being angry and bitter to being joyful and accepting in spite of her struggles. The woman was transformed by prayer—by asking, seeking, knocking. She did receive something. Maybe not what she expected, but perhaps something even better.

Some people use this verse in an effort to convince people that they ought to accept Christ. And those who haven't done that yet are labeled "seekers." If they seek, pray, and ask, they'll get saved. True enough, but I think this passage has more to say to us about deepening our connection with Jesus.

We don't just ask or knock once, get "in" with Jesus, and then coast to heaven. Right? If we do, then what are you still doing here? Still, if it's true that once we believe in Jesus, he's a part of our lives, his Spirit resides in us, and we are "saved," then what is Jesus telling us here?

I think he might be trying to remind us that faith is a journey and salvation is a life. A life lived one day at a time. A life of choices: Will we listen to the voice of love? Will we seek to do what it says? Will we love God and love others? Will we ask for God's help in living that way? Will we receive the guidance God wants to give us?

As Dallas Willard writes, "Why is it that we look upon our salvation as a moment that began our religious life instead of the daily life we receive from God?"[1]

A more accurate translation of Jesus's words in this passage might be, "everyone who keeps asking . . . keeps seeking . . . keeps knocking." According to Jesus, life with him is about continuing to seek. Not that we have to question our salvation. He promises he will never leave us or forsake us. If we believe, we'll be saved.

But I think Jesus tells us to keep seeking and keep asking because he desires a deeper relationship with us. He wants us to keep listening for the voice of love and keep responding to it. Jesus elaborates: If your child asks you for bread, do you give him a stone? If he wants fish for dinner, do you serve him a snake? If you have kids, you know what they need, but you love for them to ask you for things, to "say please." Why? Because you know that is how relationships and trust are built—by expressing needs and having them met. If they were to expect you to just figure out their needs and meet them without their ever having to ask for anything, you'd feel a bit like they were taking you for granted, wouldn't you? I think God feels the same way—he wants us to keep on conversing. Communicating our needs to God also implies that when we receive, we will be more aware of who met those needs and will say thank you.

To keep asking, seeking, and knocking is to wonder, *How can I breathe deeper? How can I walk forward in the journey and strengthen the bond with my heavenly Father?*

I don't know about you, but I haven't got life, especially life as a Christian, totally nailed just yet. I am still trying to figure it out. My primary method for this seems to be making mistakes, confessing them, and starting again. The times I do best—that is, the times I am most loving—are when I keep seeking, keep asking God for help, keep listening to his voice.

So if faith is a journey, asking Jesus to travel with us is the beginning of that journey, the birth of that new life. But it is a life of relationship, a life in which we keep asking, keep seeking, and keep knocking. And, thank God, keep receiving.

questions

What do you need to ask Jesus for in order to deepen your relationship with him?

In what ways are you a "seeker"? What is it that you are seeking?

What do you want to ask God for in your life? Do you believe that he will give it to you?

How do you think the ideas in this passage are related to Jesus's promise of an abundant life? How can they help you to breathe deeper?

Week Two Matthew 8:1–13

Jesus's Power to Heal

When Jesus came down from the mountainside, large crowds followed him. A man with leprosy came and knelt before him and said, "Lord, if you are willing, you can make me clean."

Jesus reached out his hand and touched the man. "I am willing," he said. "Be clean!" Immediately he was cleansed of his leprosy. Then Jesus said to him, "See that you don't tell anyone. But go, show yourself to the priest and offer the gift Moses commanded, as a testimony to them."

When Jesus had entered Capernaum, a centurion came to him, asking for help. "Lord," he said, "my servant lies at home paralyzed, suffering terribly."

Jesus said to him, "Shall I come and heal him?"

The centurion replied, "Lord, I do not deserve to have you come under my roof. But just say the word, and my servant will be healed. For I myself am a man under authority, with soldiers under me. I tell this one, 'Go,' and he goes; and that one, 'Come,' and he comes. I say to my servant, 'Do this,' and he does it."

When Jesus heard this, he was amazed and said to those following him, "Truly I tell you, I have not found anyone in Israel with such great faith. I say to you that many will come from the east and the west, and will take their places at the feast with Abraham, Isaac and Jacob in the kingdom of heaven. But the subjects of the kingdom will be thrown outside, into the darkness, where there will be weeping and gnashing of teeth."

Then Jesus said to the centurion, "Go! Let it be done just as you believed it would." And his servant was healed at that very hour.

Matthew 8:1–13

Day One: Deep Listening

Begin with a simple prayer: "Lord, speak to me through your Word." Sit quietly for a minute or two before you read.

Read the passage through, out loud if possible. Your instinct may be to try to compare and contrast the two healings, or you may be tempted to try to extract some lesson or solution from the text that may or may not be true, such as, "if you have enough faith, God will heal you." Resist that urge.

Instead, simply breathe in the words. Go slowly. Listen for which word or phrase leaps off the page, which word seems to demand your notice. Underline it or jot it in the margin.

Again, take a moment to be quiet. Then read through the passage again, listening again for the word that captures your attention. Take your time. What do you think God might want you to know through this word?

Let yourself enjoy the silence, reflecting on what God has said to you. After a few moments, read through the passage one more time, again looking and listening for a single word or phrase that stands out. You may hear the same word as you did in the previous reading or perhaps a different word. What is God promising or offering or asking you for through this word?

Take your life card for this week and write the word on it. If you like, add a sentence about how you want to respond to God's word to you.

Take a moment to thank God for speaking to you and to reflect on what he's said.

Day Two: Journaling

Read the text again. You may want to read it from a different translation of Scripture.[1] Imagine yourself coming to Jesus in need of healing. What needs healing in your life? What do you say to Jesus? Write for at least two minutes about what you say to Jesus (you may journal for more than two minutes, but that's a minimum). Don't edit yourself or try to phrase it just right; just let the words flow onto the paper. Don't rewrite, don't cross out, just keep your hand moving on the page and let the feelings and thoughts flow from deep within you. Don't censor yourself.

Take as much time as you want with this exercise. Don't push for an answer right away, but once you have written what you would say to Jesus, sit quietly for another few minutes. Let the question or request you've written simply sit there between you and Jesus. Trust him with it. You may want to write one insight or question from your journal on your life card.

Day Three: Being There

Read through this week's Scripture passage. What do you notice about Jesus? How would you describe him based on this passage?

We sometimes think of things we "imagine" as things that are fantasies or not true. But here you are imagining yourself in a scene that truly did happen. Now, you weren't there in actuality, but by using your imagination, you can interact with Jesus in your mind as if you were there—which is, if you think about it, how you interact with him most of the time.[2]

Imagine yourself in the scene. Let yourself daydream about it. Perhaps you are a bystander, watching Jesus. Perhaps you are the person Jesus is talking to. Put yourself into various roles in the scene. Take five or ten minutes to simply imagine the scene. Add details—what smells and sounds surround the action described? Use your five senses as you put yourself into the story: What do you see, hear, feel, taste, smell?

Imagine yourself as the leper—a person no one ever touched— being touched by Jesus. How does it feel to have a human touch after years of being deprived of that?

Describe Jesus's mood. How is he feeling? What do you imagine he is thinking?

What do you love about Jesus as you watch this scene? What confuses you or rubs you the wrong way?

By imagining yourself in the scene, you are spending time with Jesus. Don't rush to talk it over with him, but simply observe for a while.

Bring any questions or thankfulness you have to him in prayer. Simply sit with whatever comes to you for a few moments. Don't rush.

Add one sentence to your life card about what you noticed about Jesus or what he said to you as you imagined yourself in the scene.

If you'd like, read the passage to a friend or your children and ask them what they notice about Jesus, what they like about him. You may want to share your perceptions, but try to avoid sounding like you are right and they are wrong. Accept their observations; let God perhaps speak to you through them.

Sabbath Reflection

Read the text out loud. Then read slowly through this reflection. It's up to you whether to include your family or others. If you do include children, depending on their ages, you can read this to them, summarize it, or simply ask them for their observations about the story. If you have a children's Bible, you could read the story from that version. Be open to the idea that they may have some insights that God can use to speak to you. You can use the questions at the end with others or on your own. Use as many or as few of the questions as you like.

In this passage, Jesus interacts with two people. One seemed to have no power; the other appeared to be very powerful. But they had two things in common: Both were despised, and they both had faith. They had chutzpah—unusual confidence.

The leper was considered unclean by Jewish law. An unclean person had to stay away from others. He was not to touch or to be touched. Imagine the pain not only of his disease and disfigurement but also of his loneliness.

Leviticus 13 gives the Israelites rules about how to determine whether people have skin diseases and what to do about it. Read Leviticus 13:45–46. This is the law that the leper lived under. Because of his sickness, this man lived in isolation, and he had to shout out his shame whenever anyone approached.

The centurion was a Gentile and therefore despised by the Jews as well. Even worse, he was a soldier. He represented the Romans, who were in charge of the country and were not very nice about it. In fact, it was the centurion's job to enforce the rules. This soldier lived in Capernaum, Jesus's hometown, a village of Jews. He was probably not very popular. In a way, he lived in isolation as well. He didn't have to say "unclean," but when he walked on the streets, the people in the town probably gave him dirty looks and a wide berth. He may have felt a bit lonely too, I think.

Both of these men come to Jesus. Just to approach him took an enormous amount of faith. But they both trust—they have confidence that if Jesus is willing, he can change their lives. The leper says, "I know if you're willing, you can heal me" (see v. 2); the centurion says, "I know if you just say the word, my servant will be healed" (see v. 8). Both acknowledge that healing comes not from their strength or worthiness but from Jesus's generous willingness to help them.

You may not have leprosy or be a soldier for an oppressive government. But maybe you feel left out or sad or hurt sometimes. Jesus understands those feelings—I think there were times he felt lonely too. He also knows that none of us is perfect. He knows that even if we don't have a disease on our skin that people can see, we sometimes are mean or make bad choices, and that puts a disease called sin on our insides, on our hearts. He knows that sometimes we are afraid, and that keeps us from being our best. But just like Jesus healed the leper and the soldier's servant, he wants to heal us by forgiving us, if we only ask him to.

questions

What do these two men want from Jesus? What did Jesus do? How did Jesus feel about what the centurion said?

What keeps you from coming to Jesus? Do you ever feel "unclean" or unworthy? Tell about a time you were scared to talk to someone.

How did Jesus respond to people who were humble but were still courageous enough to ask him for help?

What is something you want to ask Jesus to help you with today? What attitude or pain in your life needs his healing touch?

If you have children and they are interested, you could have them try to act out this scene. Have one be a leper, one Jesus, one a soldier. Keep it light and fun—it's just an option, not required. Or, you could also offer younger children the chance to draw their answers to any of these questions.

Week Three Matthew 9:9–13

Inviting Outsiders In

Passing along, Jesus saw a man at his work collecting taxes. His name was Matthew. Jesus said, "Come along with me." Matthew stood up and followed him.

Later when Jesus was eating supper at Matthew's house with his close followers, a lot of disreputable characters came and joined them. When the Pharisees saw him keeping this kind of company, they had a fit, and lit into Jesus' followers. "What kind of example is this from your Teacher, acting cozy with crooks and riffraff?"

Jesus, overhearing, shot back, "Who needs a doctor: the healthy or the sick? Go figure out what this Scripture means: 'I'm after mercy, not religion.' I'm here to invite outsiders, not coddle insiders."

Matthew 9:9–13 Message

Day One: Deep Listening

Take a few moments to settle yourself. Take a deep breath, and release any tension in your body. Ask God to simply meet you and speak to you through this passage.

Read through the passage slowly, out loud if possible. Listen for the word or phrase that stands out to you. After you read, spend several minutes in silence. Let the word that stood out echo in your mind.

Ask God to speak to you again. Read the passage a second time, again listening for the word that jumps out at you. What does God want to remind you about or encourage you with through this word? What does he want you to know?

Spend as long as you need in silence, thinking about what God has said. When you are ready, read the passage one more time, listening again for God's word to you. Is there something he wants you to do? Is he inviting you into a deeper intimacy with himself? Is there a risk he wants you to take? Reflect on what he's said to you. You may want to write a word or sentence on your life card. Let this time lead you into a dialogue with God or a comfortable silence.

End your time by thanking him for speaking with you through his Word.

Day Two: Journaling

Matthew was a tax collector—a person despised by most Jews. Most were notorious cheats. Besides that, they were Jews but were collecting taxes on behalf of Rome.

Matthew seemed to hang with a rather raunchy crowd—other tax collectors, women of ill repute, in a word, "sinners." He was definitely not in a "holy huddle."

The point is not that Matthew needs new friends. Rather, Jesus welcomes Matthew's friends because they, like Matthew, may find themselves changed by an encounter with Jesus.

Spend some time journaling about these questions: In what ways are you like Matthew? In what ways are you different from him? If Matthew came to your church, would you advise him to get some new friends? If Jesus came to your house, what kind of people would he find? Who typically comes to your dinner parties? Who do you hang out with? What does that reveal about you? In what ways do these friends influence you or you influence them?

Day Three: Breath Prayer

Look at the word or sentence you wrote after meditating on this passage on day one. Use the word and a name for Jesus to create a single-sentence prayer that you can use throughout your day. For example, if the phrase "come along with me" touched your heart, you may want to pray something like "Jesus, guide me as I follow you." Or if the word was "mercy," you could pray something like "Jesus, have mercy on me," or "Father, help me to show your mercy to others." Take your time; let this prayer surface from your deepest, truest desires. Write your prayer on your life card and continue to pray it through the week.

Sabbath Reflection

Read the text out loud. Then read slowly through this reflection. It's up to you whether to include your family or others in this practice. If you do include children, depending on their ages, you can read this to them, summarize it, or simply ask them for their observations about the story. If you have a children's Bible, you could read the story from that version. Be open to the idea that they may have some insights that God can use to speak to you. You can use the questions at the end with others or on your own. Use as many or as few of the questions as you like.

To us, Jesus's way of gathering his team of disciples may seem strange. He seems to wander up to ordinary people (not society's best and brightest, by the way) and just say, "Follow me." And they do it. (See also Matthew 4:18–22 or Luke 5:1–11 for the calling of four other disciples.)

While we may marvel at how quickly these young men left their day jobs to follow Jesus, we need to understand that in Jesus's culture, it was an amazing honor to have a rabbi invite you to be a disciple.

In fact, typically only those who were considered the top religious students would even be considered for the privilege and honor of being a disciple or apprentice of a rabbi. And they would always approach the rabbi and ask for the privilege of being allowed to follow and learn from him. If the rabbi accepted them as disciples, they would spend as much time as possible with him, trying to learn by watching and listening. But typically rabbis simply didn't ask people to follow them. That would be like Donald Trump showing up at your door to invite you to be his "apprentice" without you having to apply for it or go through the competition.

Jesus does not pick the people you'd expect—he seems to take the leftovers, the bottom rather than the top of the class. He chooses those who need him. To those who question his method, Jesus says, "Who needs a doctor: the healthy or the sick?" (see v. 12).

I'm someone whose soul needs doctoring. Even as I'm following him, I've got a long way to go before perfection sets in, believe me.

It's interesting that the religious establishment criticizes Jesus's method. But they don't question him directly. Instead they attack these relatively new disciples, who aren't exactly the valedictorians of Hebrew school.

But Jesus steps in. And he quotes a verse from the Old Testament, which would seem to us to be a bit of a smack on the Pharisees. But it was rabbi code for something even more insulting. See, as part of their religious training, the Pharisees and Jesus would have had the Old Testament memorized. If you quoted one verse to them, they could tell you what the verses before and after it said. So one verse would remind them of an entire passage.

Look at the context of Jesus's comment in verse 13, which comes from Hosea 6:6. In that passage God says to his stubborn, unrepentant people, "Your love is like the morning mist, like the early dew that disappears. Therefore I cut you in pieces with my prophets, I killed you with the words of my mouth; my judgments flashed like lightning upon you. For I desire mercy, not sacrifice" (Hosea 6:4–6 NIV).

Apparently Jesus had not read *How to Win Friends and Influence People*. When he says he has not come to call "the righteous," it seems he is really saying "the *self*-righteous."

Jesus invites sinners, people who do not have their act together, to come and join the party. To be a part of what he's doing.

Jesus extends to each of us the same invitation he gave to those Galilean fishermen and to Matthew: "Come along with me." We accept or decline the invitation not just once but daily.

questions

If you'd been Matthew, how would you have felt when Jesus came up to you at work and said, "Follow me"?

What do you think Jesus talked about with the people at Matthew's dinner party? Jesus said he came to heal people who were spiritually sick. How might those people have been changed by encountering Jesus? Do you ever hang around with people who are different from you?

What does it mean for you to follow him today? What choices will you make to follow him more closely?

Week Four

Matthew 10:1–20

Sending Out Rookies

Jesus called his twelve disciples to him and gave them authority to drive out evil spirits and to heal every disease and sickness.

These are the names of the twelve apostles: first, Simon (who is called Peter) and his brother Andrew; James son of Zebedee, and his brother John; Philip and Bartholomew; Thomas and Matthew the tax collector; James son of Alphaeus, and Thaddaeus; Simon the Zealot and Judas Iscariot, who betrayed him.

These twelve Jesus sent out with the following instructions: "Do not go among the Gentiles or enter any town of the Samaritans. Go rather to the lost sheep of Israel. As you go, proclaim this message: 'The kingdom of heaven has come near.' Heal the sick, raise the dead, cleanse those who have leprosy, drive out demons. Freely you have received, freely give.

"Do not get any gold or silver or copper to take with you in your belts—no bag for the journey or extra shirt or sandals or a staff, for workers are worth their keep. Whatever town or village you enter, search for some worthy person there and stay at that person's house until you leave. As you enter the home, give it your greeting. If the home is deserving, let your peace rest on it; if it is not, let your peace return to you. If anyone will not welcome you or listen to your words, shake the dust off

your feet when you leave that home or town. Truly I tell you, it will be more bearable for Sodom and Gomorrah on the day of judgment than for that town.

"I am sending you out like sheep among wolves. Therefore be as shrewd as snakes and as innocent as doves. Be on your guard; you will be handed over to the local councils and be flogged in the synagogues. On my account you will be brought before governors and kings as witnesses to them and to the Gentiles. But when they arrest you, do not worry about what to say or how to say it. At that time you will be given what to say, for it will not be you speaking, but the Spirit of your Father speaking through you."

Matthew 10:1–20

Day One: Being There

Read slowly through the passage. In this practice, remember, you are using your imagination to enter the story as a way of spending time with Jesus. Create a short video in your mind, watching the scene unfold. Put yourself into various roles in the scene. Take five or ten minutes to simply imagine the scene, to "daydream" about it. Add details—what smells and sounds surround the action described? Use your five senses as you put yourself into the story: What do you see, hear, feel, taste, smell?

This passage has a list of the twelve disciples. Pick one and imagine you are that person, being instructed by Jesus. How do you feel? Jesus is telling you to heal people and drive out demons—but not giving a lot of specific instructions on how to do that. Are you nervous, excited, fearful?

What do you notice about Jesus? What surprises you about him? What questions do you wish you could ask him? You may want to jot some observations or questions on your life card or in your journal. End your meditation by thanking Jesus for the opportunity to spend some time with him.

Day Two: Kindness

It's interesting that Jesus's instructions to his disciples about what to *say* are much shorter than his instructions about what to *do*. Apparently, telling people "the kingdom of heaven is near" won't mean much without the actions of healing and blessing—one follows the other. We may not be able to heal someone of leprosy; I don't think I even know anyone with leprosy. But there are plenty of people with other afflictions, such as AIDS. We can extend kindness and healing to them—we can't fix their problem overnight, but perhaps we can take some small step by learning more about their problems. It may be by something as simple as supporting an organization such as World Vision that is working in areas ravaged by this disease or as radical as visiting a hospital and praying for people.

Later in the passage, Jesus warns his disciples that some people may not like what they are doing. They may question them, even arrest them. He tells his disciples to trust that the Spirit will give them words to say. Again, actions of trust and kindness are more important than preparing speeches.

How can you show people with your actions that the kingdom of heaven is near? What is God asking you to give? Take a step to give it.

Day Three: Solitude

Solitude is simply time alone with God. Finding that time can sometimes be anything but simple. Make arrangements to get some time alone. Get out of the house; turn off your cell phone. If you have small children, perhaps you will want to have a friend watch them at your house while you go to *her* house, where you will be less tempted to do chores or answer the phone.

45

Don't bring much—maybe this book and your Bible. Notice that in this passage Jesus tells his disciples not to bring a bunch of stuff. Let that be your instruction for your time of solitude. Don't bring a stack of books, tapes, Bible studies, and so on. This is time for you to be quiet with God.

Spend as long as you need just sitting still. Take some time to just breathe slowly and deeply. Release tension, ask God to meet you, then wait. When you find yourself distracted, allow your wandering thoughts to simply float away from you. Trust that your to-do list will still be there when you return.

Once you're able to feel yourself quieting down, you may want to read through the passage. Spend some time reflecting on Jesus's statement, "Freely you have received, freely give" (v. 8). What have you received? Take some time to be grateful, really grateful. What can you give? Ask God to help you to be generous.

Sabbath Reflection

Read the text out loud. Then read slowly through this reflection. It's up to you whether to include your family or others in this practice. If you do include children, depending on their ages, you can read this to them, summarize it, or simply ask them for their observations about the story. If you have a children's Bible, you could read the story from that version. Be open to the idea that they may have some insights that God can use to speak to you. You can use the questions at the end with others or on your own. Use as many or as few of the questions as you like.

Several years ago I was invited to speak at a large women's conference. That would have been fine, except that at that time, I hated public speaking and wasn't very good at it. This is not false modesty. Really. Ask someone who was there: I was mediocre at best when it came to speaking. I've improved a bit in the meantime, but then—let's just say it wasn't my strong suit.

Well, when the invitation came, I happened to be reading John Ortberg's book *If You Want to Walk on Water, You've Got to Get Out of the Boat.* This assignment felt like walking on water to me—except I knew I would not walk, I would sink like a rock. But I read, "Is there any challenge in your life right now that is large enough that you have no hope of doing it apart from God's help? If not, consider the possibility that you are seriously underchallenged."[1]

Feeling like the words were written from God to me, I reluctantly said yes to the speaking gig. And I got through it, despite challenges. I know God spoke through me to one gal there who stopped me in the hallway, tears in her eyes. I also know I bored or confused quite a few other people, according to their ruthless seminar evaluations. Sigh.

But I obeyed. I did something I could not do without a generous measure of God's help. And my faith grew. (Thankfully, with some training, my public speaking skills improved as well, so that now when I speak at conferences, I can be a bit more helpful.)

Jesus said to his disciples, "I am sending you out like sheep among wolves. Therefore be as shrewd as snakes and as innocent as doves" (v. 16).

Sheep are not very smart and are quite vulnerable, especially when they find themselves among wolves. (Wolves with seminar evaluations are especially bloodthirsty, I might add.) You're dead meat, really. That, said Jesus, is how you will feel sometimes. Jesus gave his disciples this assignment: Preach a one-sentence sermon, and then "heal the sick, raise the dead," he tells them almost casually (v. 8). Can you see the disciples looking at him like he's nuts and saying, "Sure, no problem, and while we're at it, we'll cast out demons too"? "Good," Jesus replies. "Now we're on the same page—thanks for reminding me about that one."

How are the disciples supposed to do this? Then Jesus adds, "Oh, and don't take any supplies or money with you; rely on the kindness of strangers to take you in and feed you, although you have to expect that not everyone will welcome you. And you'll probably get arrested, maybe beaten, and questioned. So in addition to being a sheep, be like a snake and also like a dove."

Snakes are smart and crafty, able to wriggle their way out of sticky situations, I guess. Doves are gentle, a symbol of peace. The disciples will need to be both. Underchallenged, they will not be. They have no hope of success—except, Jesus says, that the Spirit will be with them and will give them words to say.

This is still true today. Jesus may not be asking you to raise the dead. But is he asking you to share your faith with someone who is spiritually comatose, to offer them life? Is he asking you to heal the heart of someone who is discouraged, simply by listening to them and praying for them?

The kingdom of heaven is near; that's the message he calls all of his disciples (including you and me) to share. We can't do it without his help—which is exactly the point, isn't it?

questions

How would you respond to the question from John Ortberg's book: "Is there any challenge in your life right now that is large enough that you have no hope of doing it apart from God's help?"

Why do you think Jesus tells his disciples not to take any money or supplies as they go out to preach, to heal, and to cast out demons?

What assignment do you sense Jesus is calling you to take on right now? What is keeping you from obeying?

Tell about a time you risked failure and found that you were able to accomplish something with God's help. How did that affect your faith?

Week Five Matthew 12:1–14

Lord of the Sabbath

At that time Jesus went through the grainfields on the Sabbath. His disciples were hungry and began to pick some heads of grain and eat them. When the Pharisees saw this, they said to him, "Look! Your disciples are doing what is unlawful on the Sabbath."

He answered, "Haven't you read what David did when he and his companions were hungry? He entered the house of God, and he and his companions ate the consecrated bread—which was not lawful for them to do, but only for the priests. Or haven't you read in the Law that the priests on Sabbath duty in the temple desecrate the Sabbath and yet are innocent? I tell you that one greater than the temple is here. If you had known what these words mean, 'I desire mercy, not sacrifice,' you would not have condemned the innocent. For the Son of Man is Lord of the Sabbath."

Going on from that place, he went into their synagogue, and a man with a shriveled hand was there. Looking for a reason to accuse Jesus, they asked him, "Is it lawful to heal on the Sabbath?"

He said to them, "If any of you has a sheep and it falls into a pit on the Sabbath, will you not take hold of it and lift it out? How much more valuable is a human being than a sheep! Therefore it is lawful to do good on the Sabbath."

Then he said to the man, "Stretch out your hand." So he stretched it out and it was completely restored, just as sound as the other. But the Pharisees went out and plotted how they might kill Jesus.

Matthew 12:1–14

Day One: Deep Listening

Take a few moments to settle yourself. Take a deep breath, and release any tension in your body. Ask God to simply meet you and speak to you through this passage.

Read through the passage slowly, out loud if possible. Listen for the word or phrase that stands out to you. After you read, spend several minutes in silence. Let the word that stood out echo in your mind.

This passage can easily be divided into two sections: verses 1–8 and verses 9–14. After reading the whole thing, you may choose to focus on just one of these sections, if you like. Let the Spirit guide your reading.

Ask God to speak to you again. Read the passage a second time, again listening for the word that jumps out at you. What is God wanting to remind you about or encourage you with through this word? What does he want you to know?

Spend as long as you need in silence, thinking about what God has said. When you are ready, read the passage one more time, listening again for God's word to you. Is there something he wants you to do? Is he inviting you into a deeper intimacy with himself? Is there a risk he wants you to take? Reflect on what he's said to you. Let this time lead you into a dialogue with God or a comfortable silence.

End your time by thanking him for speaking with you through his Word.

Day Two: Breath Prayer

Read the passage again, slowly. In this passage, Jesus is misunderstood and criticized. His detractors are so angry with him for not doing things the way they think they ought to be done that they want to kill him.

I feel for Jesus, but I'm also glad that he knows what it is like to be misunderstood, to be attacked for what he said and did. I've experienced that and it's not fun, but it helps to know that Jesus understands and has, in fact, had it worse than I have.

Do you feel misunderstood? Is there pain in your life? Use this time of prayer to bring that to Jesus. He not only understands your feelings, he's experienced the same kind of pain, the pain of being misunderstood. Ask him to gently show you if you are doing something to cause your own pain or if you are too concerned about other people's opinions. This may be the case, or it may not. Ask for clarity about your motives and your actions. Be still. Listen. What do you need from Jesus? Perhaps it is reassurance or comfort. Put that need into a single-sentence prayer, such as "Jesus, comfort me," or "Lord, your grace is sufficient for me." Spend some time simply praying that sentence, then falling silent. Write the prayer on your life card and take it with you through your week.

Day Three: Journaling

Jesus seems to get into trouble quite frequently over his differences of opinion with the Pharisees, especially regarding what's allowed on the Sabbath. As he did in the passage we looked at in week two (see Matt. 9:9–13), Jesus again quotes one of his favorite Old Testament passages, Hosea 6:6: "I desire mercy, not sacrifice." Write these words on your life card and in your

51

journal. Spend some time just writing about what you think this means in your own life.

When we read about the Pharisees in the Bible, we're often tempted to look down our noses at them, to wonder why they just didn't get it. But their stories are included in the Bible not so we can feel superior to them, but to remind us that we are just like them. Journal a bit about the following questions: Where are you tempted to make your faith about rules? As you've tried to begin to practice Sabbath, how have you been tempted to make up some "rules" about it?

Sabbath Reflection

Read this week's text out loud. Then read slowly through this reflection. It's up to you whether to include your family or others in this practice. If you do include children, depending on their ages, you can read this to them, summarize it, or simply ask them for their observations about the story. If you have a children's Bible, you could read the story from that version. Be open to the idea that they may have some insights that God can use to speak to you. You can use the questions at the end with others or on your own. Use as many or as few of the questions as you like.

Today our Sabbath Reflection is on the topic of the Sabbath. The Pharisees were very concerned with what was "lawful." What fit within the rules?

The Jews lived in a land occupied by Rome. The Torah, God's law, stood in direct opposition to the pantheistic, permissive culture of Rome. Following God's rules was what made the Jews holy—set apart and different from the non-Jews around them who might worship gods whose temples had "temple prostitutes" or believe in any number of gods.

In some ways, the Pharisees are similar to some conservative Christians today, who want their behavior to stand in sharp contrast to the culture around them. After all, the Bible tells us, "Do not conform any longer to the pattern of this world, but be transformed by the renewing of your mind" (Rom. 12:2 NIV). If our minds are transformed, our attitudes and actions will also be changed. We'll try to act as Jesus would.

The Jews of Jesus's day also wanted to be transformed. They wanted to delight in God's law so that their lives would be fruitful (see Psalm 1). The law, the rules, had come from God. God had given his people the Torah, the law, saying, "Here's a better way to live. Don't just go along with the sexually permissive, theologically confused, morally relativistic culture that surrounds you. Be holy, set apart, different." That's good, right? God still calls us to live in a way that is different. Christians should not be known for drunkenness, promiscuity, or cheating on their taxes, right? It was the same for the Jews of Jesus's day. They wanted to live according to God's way, not the way of the culture.

A huge part of living out that faith was keeping the Sabbath. It was a highly visible way for Jews to be "different" from the culture around them. While the Torah had specifics about the rules for Sabbath, over the years rabbis had added their own stipulations about what it meant to "work" and therefore what was prohibited and allowed: how far you could walk on the Sabbath, what you could carry or not, all kinds of rules.

Again, this was not necessarily a bad thing. Structure, guidelines—these help us live holy lives. So it makes sense that the Pharisees say to Jesus, "Your disciples are doing what is unlawful on the Sabbath" (v. 2) and "Is it lawful to heal on the Sabbath?" (v. 10). Their concern is with the law. What's lawful? What's okay? They worried that people following Jesus, becoming his disciples, and wanting to live out the Torah the way he says to might be led astray. The Pharisees were conservatives who seemed worried that Jesus was a flaming liberal, that his interpretation of

Scripture was just a bit too loose. I wonder if they talked about Jesus leading people down a "slippery slope" of immorality.

Jesus wasn't just trying to be difficult or to get the Pharisees to lighten up. However, he was pointing out that their focus had shifted from God to the rules. And now he was ushering in a whole new thing. The kingdom of God, he said, was at hand, was here. It was a new day. Jesus was more concerned with the spirit of the law than the letter. Jesus's interpretation of the law went back to its original intent, which was to foster relationship with God. His way was simple: "Love God and love others." That's it.

Love was, and is, Jesus's supreme value. He told his followers, It's about love. It's about mercy, rather than sacrifices that are prescribed by law. That's how you breathe deeper, that's how you get this abundant life that I'm inviting you to live. The Sabbath is not about technicalities. It's about people. "How much more valuable is a human being than a sheep?" Jesus asks before he heals the man with a shriveled hand (Matt. 12:12).

It's easy for me to look down my nose at the Pharisees and their haughty attitude. But this story, if I let it speak to me, asks me this: Does the way I practice my faith flow out of a love for God and others or out of a sense of obligation and rule-keeping? How do I treat others who may not live the same lifestyle I do?

questions

What "rules" are a part of your faith? What choices do you make to be different from the culture around you?

What is one change you would like to make to your lifestyle to align it more closely with God's reminder, "I desire mercy, not sacrifice" (Hosea 6:6)? In other words, how can you live a more merciful life?

Where have you been shown mercy? Who in your life needs you to show mercy to them?

Week Six

Going for a Walk

Immediately Jesus made the disciples get into the boat and go on ahead of him to the other side, while he dismissed the crowd. After he had dismissed them, he went up on a mountainside by himself to pray. When evening came, he was there alone, but the boat was already a considerable distance from land, buffeted by the waves because the wind was against it.

Shortly before dawn Jesus went out to them, walking on the lake. When the disciples saw him walking on the lake, they were terrified. "It's a ghost," they said, and cried out in fear.

But Jesus immediately said to them: "Take courage! It is I. Don't be afraid."

"Lord, if it's you," Peter replied, "tell me to come to you on the water."

"Come," he said.

Then Peter got down out of the boat, walked on the water and came toward Jesus. But when he saw the wind, he was afraid and, beginning to sink, cried out, "Lord, save me!"

Immediately Jesus reached out his hand and caught him. "You of little faith," he said, "why did you doubt?"

And when they climbed into the boat, the wind died down. Then those who were in the boat worshiped him, saying, "Truly you are the Son of God."

When they had crossed over, they landed at Gennesaret. And when the men of that place recognized Jesus, they sent word to all the surrounding country. People brought all their sick to him and begged him to let the sick just touch the edge of his cloak, and all who touched him were healed.

Matthew 14:22–36

Day One: Breath Prayer

Remember, a breath prayer is a single-sentence prayer, one
that can be prayed in the space of a single breath. It combines
an intimate name for God with our deepest spiritual desire.

Read slowly through the passage. Imagine you are there. Listen
in on Jesus's conversation with Peter. Which of Peter's statements
resonates with you? Make that statement your prayer. Perhaps
you will want to pray, "Lord, tell me to come to you." Or "Lord,
save me!" You may not be taking a stroll across a lake, literally,
but perhaps you're facing a challenge. Perhaps you need Jesus
to take you by the hand and keep you from sinking. When you
pray, imagine that you are walking toward Jesus, ready to grab
his hand if you should begin to sink.

Once you have your prayer, sit quietly. Take several slow,
deep breaths in silence. Then pray the prayer in the space of
one breath. Sit in silence. When your mind wanders, use the
prayer to focus again, in the space of a slow inhale and exhale.
Breathe in God's presence and his touch; breathe out your fear
or concern.

Write down your sentence prayer and any other notes on
your life card.

Day Two: Deep Listening

Take a few moments to settle yourself. Take a deep breath,
and release any tension in your body. Ask God to simply meet
you and speak to you through this passage.

Read through the passage slowly, out loud if possible. Listen
for the word or phrase that stands out to you. After you read,
spend several minutes in silence. Let the word that stood out
echo in your mind.

Ask God to speak to you again. Read the passage a second time, again listening for the word that jumps out at you. What is God wanting to remind you about or encourage you with through this word? What does he want you to know?

Spend as long as you need in silence, thinking about what God has said. When you are ready, read the passage one more time, listening again for God's word to you. Is there something he wants you to do? Is he inviting you into a deeper intimacy with himself? Is there a risk he wants you to take? Reflect on what he's said to you. Let this time lead you into a dialogue with God or a comfortable silence.

Jot a sentence or two on your life card.

End your time by thanking him for speaking with you through his Word.

Day Three: Solitude

Make arrangements to get by yourself for at least a half hour—longer if possible. If you have small children, you may use nap time, but getting out of the house is optimum.

Take some time to just be quiet. List some things you are grateful for on your life card or in your journal.

Read the passage again. Where has God met you this week through this passage? What insights did you gain from the earlier exercises? Spend some time thanking him for that.

Spend part of your solitude time simply listening to God and listening to your life. What challenges did you face this week in which you felt like you were being asked to walk on water? What might God be trying to teach you through those challenges? Be honest: Have those difficulties increased your trust in Jesus or hindered your faith? Don't get mired in guilt; simply be honest with God and ask him for whatever help you need—just as Peter did when he started to sink.

Sabbath Reflection

Read the text out loud. Then read slowly through this reflection. It's up to you whether to include your family or others in this practice. If you do include children, depending on their ages, you can read this to them, summarize it, or simply ask them for their observations about the story. If you have a children's Bible, you could read the story from that version. Be open to the idea that they may have some insights that God can use to speak to you. You can use the questions at the end with others or on your own. Use as many or as few of the questions as you like.

In my worn, taped, marked-up old Bible, the phrase "he went up on a mountainside by himself to pray" (v. 23 NIV) is highlighted. Earlier in the chapter, I've underlined the phrase "he withdrew by boat privately to a solitary place" (v. 13).

If you read the whole of Matthew 14, you'll see that in the few days before he walks on water, Jesus has been through quite a lot.

He learns that his cousin John the Baptist, a very important person in his life, has been senselessly killed. He tries to get away—to grieve, perhaps. When Jesus heard about John's beheading, he withdrew to a solitary place. But people followed, interrupting his attempts at solitude. He'd gone by boat, hoping to avoid them, but they followed on foot, figuring out where he'd land.

Jesus had compassion; he loved people. He met their needs, miraculously turning a few loaves and fishes into a feast. But he knew how to set boundaries. Sometimes I feel guilty for taking time alone—for spending time just sitting with Jesus when everyone else around me is busy and frantic.

There is a time to offer compassion, to meet needs and feed people, both physically and spiritually. But there is also a time to withdraw, to be alone. To grieve, maybe, or just to breathe.

Part of my work in the world involves leading retreats and speaking to groups. Sometimes I get to travel to do this, which I love. Yet while I enjoy teaching and interacting with people, my introvert personality needs some solitude to recover from the intensity of that kind of ministry.

When I first started traveling to speak, I would hurry straight home after the retreat (often because my family would insist that I ought to), only to be thrown into the chaos of a family that had missed me (but hadn't done the laundry while I was gone). Depleted as I was, it was hard to meet those needs, and I found I would crave time alone, which was even harder to find because I'd been gone for a couple of days.

Last fall I led a retreat near Phoenix. I have a writer friend in that city. I told her I'd be in town. Diane and her husband were going to be gone the day the retreat ended but would be back the next day. But they graciously offered to let me stay at their home. It was an unexpected blessing—a time of solitude and prayer.

I'd loved the retreat—the women from Anthem Fellowship were wonderful. But as usual after a weekend of speaking and processing with women, I craved rest and soul replenishment.

The time alone was a gift—from my friend but also from God, who knew I needed just a little time to rest and also to think about my ministry, my family, and how to fit the needs of both together into a life.

I'd been invited to write another book (which you are now reading). I listened, I prayed. Jesus and I brainstormed about a different kind of devotional and what that might look like. I wrote a preliminary outline, prayed, rewrote the outline. I let myself daydream about what the book would look like. What if it had structure but freedom? What if it were a tool but not a burden? How could I write it in a way that would allow God to speak louder than I did?

It wasn't easy, taking that extra day. My family would have preferred that I come straight home. But sometimes we have to follow Jesus into that solitary place. He had to let the needs of the crowds, even of his disciples, go unmet for a little while. Sometimes, I think, we must do the same: dismiss the crowd and go to a solitary place to pray.

Now when I travel to speak, I will sometimes add an extra day for myself, to recover in solitude—even if it's the solitude of exploring a city by myself, sitting in a café reading or writing. Sometimes it's replenishing, and sometimes there are moments when I feel sort of lonely. Either way, it throws me into conversation with Jesus.

While you may not have the opportunity to travel for your job, you can dismiss the crowd of your family and go, at least once in a while, to a solitary place to pray, to listen, to breathe deeper for just a little while.

questions

How often do you take time to get away? Why do you suppose Jesus made this a regular practice?

How do you think the people around you (family, friends, co-workers) will respond if you try to make time for solitude? Will they follow you with their needs? Do you know for sure, or are you just imagining their response? How can you begin to set the boundaries needed for solitude?

What do you think Jesus prayed about that night? How did he know he ought to go to his disciples out on the lake?

Week Seven   Matthew 20:20-28

A Mom's Foolish Request

It was about that time that the mother of the Zebedee brothers came with her two sons and knelt before Jesus with a request.

"What do you want?" Jesus asked.

She said, "Give your word that these two sons of mine will be awarded the highest places of honor in your kingdom, one at your right hand, one at your left hand."

Jesus responded, "You have no idea what you're asking." And he said to James and John, "Are you capable of drinking the cup that I'm about to drink?"

They said, "Sure, why not?"

Jesus said, "Come to think of it, you are going to drink my cup. But as to awarding places of honor, that's not my business. My Father is taking care of that."

When the ten others heard about this, they lost their tempers, thoroughly disgusted with the two brothers. So Jesus got them together to settle things down. He said, "You've observed how godless rulers throw their weight around, how quickly a little power goes to their heads. It's not going to be that way with you. Whoever wants to be great must become a servant. Whoever wants to be first among you must be your slave. That is what the Son of Man has done: He came to serve, not be served—and then to give away his life in exchange for the many who are held hostage."

Matthew 20:20–28 Message

Day One: Being There

Read slowly through the passage. In this practice, remember, you are using your imagination to enter the story as a way of spending time with Jesus. Create a short video in your mind, watching the scene unfold. Put yourself into various roles in the scene. Take five or ten minutes to simply imagine the scene, to "daydream" about it. Add details—what smells and sounds surround the action described? Use your five senses as you put yourself into the story: What do you see, hear, feel, taste, smell?

Imagine that you are James and John's mother. Why do you make this request? How do you feel about it? The text says the two young men were with their mom but let her do the talking at first. Imagine the conversation between this mom and her boys just a few minutes before they go to Jesus. Do they put her up to it, or do you think it was her idea?

What do you notice about Jesus in this scene? How would you describe him?

Imagine yourself as one of the other disciples. What are you feeling at first? What do you think about after Jesus calls you together and tells you that in order to be great, you will have to be a servant?

Day Two: Breath Prayer

You'll need to get some time of quiet, alone. You may want to plan ahead to get up early or set aside part of your day.

Read slowly through the text again. Select a word or phrase that expresses your love to Jesus, either from the text (for example, "servant") or from your observation of him (perhaps "patient"). Sit quietly. Allow yourself to be present with Jesus, to feel the love you have for him. When your mind wanders or you get distracted, pray the word or phrase again to draw you gently back into his presence. Move beyond conversation to communion, simply being with him. If you like, write your prayer on your life card. Pray it again throughout the week.

Day Three: Kindness

In this passage, Jesus tries to help his disciples see that his kingdom is not like other kingdoms. The power structure is different, the organizational chart is just about upside down. If you want to become great, Jesus says, then become a servant.

Today, find a way to become great in Jesus's kingdom. Ask God to show you who needs to be served—maybe a friend or neighbor who just had a new baby and needs some help cleaning her house. Maybe you know someone who needs to have some time alone—offer to watch her children.

Maybe it's your own family that needs someone to serve them, but God is asking you to see it as a way of furthering the kingdom of God, rather than drudgery. What could you do as Jesus's ambassador today? Perhaps it's something you need to do anyway that can be transformed by your attitude and sense of purpose.

Sabbath Reflection

Read this week's text out loud. Then read slowly through this reflection. It's up to you whether to include your family or others in this practice. If you do include children, depending on their ages, you can read this to them, summarize it, or simply ask them for their observations about the story. If you have a children's Bible, you could read the story from that version. Be open to the idea that they may have some

*insights that God can use to speak to you. You can use the questions
at the end with others or on your own. Use as many or as few of the
questions as you like.*

When I read this story, I tend to identify with the other disciples: I'm indignant. Who are these sons of Zebedee? Who do they think they are?

Well, who *did* they think they were?

In Matthew 4:18–22, we read about Jesus inviting two sets of brothers to be among his disciples. First Simon and his brother Andrew, then James and John, the sons of Zebedee.

As we learned in week three, it was an unheard-of honor to be invited by a rabbi to be a disciple. Typically it was a position only the best and the brightest dared apply for.

Maybe the fact that Jesus chose them, selected them to be among the first of his disciples, gave them the idea that they were important. Who did they think they were? They thought (correctly) that they were honored, chosen, special.

Jesus had many disciples; that is, men and women who followed him—learning from him, emulating his actions, putting their faith in him, even supporting his ministry (see Luke 8:1–3). Of those disciples, twelve were chosen to be "apostles," sort of higher-up apprentices who could go out and teach and preach, even heal and cast out demons (see Matthew 10 and week four).

James and John were not only invited to be disciples but also selected as apostles and given supernatural power to do what Jesus did. They were divinely appointed to be a part of Jesus's ministry. I'm guessing that these two experienced a deep intimacy with Jesus as well.

So it's understandable, I suppose, that they might have assumed, "Okay, you chose us as disciples, and then we made the cut for apostles. We're advancing." And then Jesus took them, with only one other disciple, Peter, up on a mountain for an amazing experience—the transfiguration (see Matt.

17:1–11). If you read the Gospels, you see fairly clearly that Peter, James, and John were Jesus's closest friends, his inner circle, if you will.

So maybe their request is not so outrageous. They'd been moving up, or so it seemed to them. Why not ask for the number two slot if you are already in the top three, or so it seems? If Jesus were running a corporation or a traditional kingdom, this would make perfect sense. Only he's not. So it doesn't.

But this desire for recognition, this wanting to be important—if I really pay attention, I'll find that I have that in me too. It's great to be able to write and be published, but wouldn't it be nice if one of my books became a best-seller? It's wonderful to have opportunities to teach, but wouldn't it be wonderful to be a renowned and sought-after speaker?

I realize this is not a very humble attitude, but it's something all of us, we must admit if we are honest, think about at least some of the time. Maybe that's why I get a little indignant. It's a way of avoiding the uncomfortable truth: James and John remind me of myself. I mean, most of the time, I can be content with the assignment Jesus has given me. Sometimes, unfortunately, I'm tempted, like James and John, to assume that the gift of Christ's intimate friendship would bring recognition for my amazing spiritual maturity. I want more.

Maybe you want people to think you're supermom, or a great wife, or just so amazing at juggling your family with your career. Maybe you wish the pastor would mention from the pulpit what a great job you're doing on your committee at church.

Even if we're not climbing a career ladder, all of us long for significance and recognition. Jesus understands that—but then reminds us that our significance comes not from position or power but from being loved and chosen by him. And when we really believe in that love, it will change our hearts and make us want to love others in the way Jesus loves us—by serving.

We've been given the gift of intimacy with Christ. We have been chosen. But we may not receive fame or accolades from other people. Our privilege is to be like the one we follow: to serve others and show them his love.

questions

What do you think motivated James, John, and their mother to make this request?

Is there an area in your life where you wish you could get a little more recognition or advancement—perhaps at work or in the work you do at home?

What is one step you could take to begin to live out Jesus's command to serve others?

Week Eight Mark 1:21–39

Finding a Rhythm
of Work and Rest

They went to Capernaum, and when the Sabbath came, Jesus went into the synagogue and began to teach. The people were amazed at his teaching, because he taught them as one who had authority, not as the teachers of the law. Just then a man in their synagogue who was possessed by an evil spirit cried out, "What do you want with us, Jesus of Nazareth? Have you come to destroy us? I know who you are—the Holy One of God!"

"Be quiet!" said Jesus sternly. "Come out of him!" The evil spirit shook the man violently and came out of him with a shriek.

The people were all so amazed that they asked each other, "What is this? A new teaching—and with authority! He even gives orders to evil spirits and they obey him." News about him spread quickly over the whole region of Galilee.

As soon as they left the synagogue, they went with James and John to the home of Simon and Andrew. Simon's mother-in-law was in bed with a fever, and they immediately told Jesus about her. So he went to her, took her hand and helped her up. The fever left her and she began to wait on them.

That evening after sunset the people brought to Jesus all the sick and demon-possessed. The whole town gathered at the door, and Jesus healed *many who had various diseases. He also drove out many demons, but he would not let the demons speak because they knew who he was.*

Very early in the morning, while it was still dark, Jesus got up, left the house and went off to a solitary place, where he prayed. Simon and his companions went to look for him, and when they found him, they exclaimed: "Everyone is looking for you!"

Jesus replied, "Let us go somewhere else—to the nearby villages—so I can preach there also. That is why I have come." So he traveled throughout Galilee, preaching in their synagogues and driving out demons.

Mark 1:21–39

Day One: Being There

Read through the text. This is a description of a typical weekend in Jesus's life. Observe each of the three scenes as they unfold.

Imagine you are there, watching Jesus as he teaches and heals in the synagogue. What are people saying about him? What comments do you overhear? Do you sense energy and excitement in the air? How does it feel to be in the crowded synagogue? How do you suppose Jesus is feeling?

Observe Jesus as he comes to Simon Peter's house. Who is there? While she isn't mentioned, Simon's wife was likely there—you don't have a mother-in-law unless you've got a wife. Peter seemed to be spending most of his time with Jesus. How to you think his wife felt about that? Is there a bit of tension between Peter and his wife?

Use your imagination to paint the scene: What was the house like? How did they spend their Sabbath? The Sabbath ended at sunset—and that's when Jesus went back to work healing people, ministering to them. Imagine yourself as one of the people coming to Jesus in the late evening or one of those privileged to have spent a Sabbath day with him.

Watch Jesus as he slips out of the house early the next morning to be alone with his Father. How is he feeling? How does he respond when his solitude is interrupted? What do you love about Jesus? What rubs you the wrong way? What questions do you have?

If you feel drawn to one particular scene, spend more time on that one. Jot one or two things that you notice about Jesus on your life card.

Day Two: Journaling

Read Isaiah 35:3–6, which is an Old Testament prophecy about the Messiah, the one whom prophets said would come to save Israel. Write this Scripture in your journal. Which word or phrase expresses a current need in your life? For example, do you have a fearful heart? Do you feel like you need strength? Write a prayer in your journal based on that word or phrase. For example, you may simply write, "Lord, strengthen my feeble hands. Give me the strength to serve my family when I'm tired."

Now read this week's text again.

The people around Jesus in Capernaum would have been familiar with the words in Isaiah. What do you think they thought about Jesus? Who did they think he was? Who do you think he was?

Journal about this for a few minutes. Select one verse from this week's reading or from the passage in Isaiah and write it on your life card. Read and say it over to yourself throughout the week, or over the next few weeks, until you have it memorized.

Day Three: Solitude

Read just Mark 1:35–37. Read it slowly a few times. You know the context: Jesus has been busy. Part of the full life he promised, we can find by doing what he did. He modeled for us a way of life. If Jesus needed solitude, you do too. It won't be easy—even Jesus was interrupted with "Everyone is looking for you!" (v. 37). Does this ever happen to you? Think about the fact that Jesus knows what you're going through—he was interrupted too.

But that didn't stop him from spending time alone. Today, slip away. If you have small children, arrange for a friend or relative to watch them—with the promise you'll return the favor. It's okay to do this. You're putting on your oxygen mask so that ultimately, you can help your kids.

Find a place where you can be quiet and alone—a park, a library, maybe your car. I know someone who, when she needs time alone to write, goes to the bride's room at her church, which is often unused during the week and has no phone and no Internet access. Be creative in finding a quiet space.

Pray quietly. Prayer is not just talking; it's also listening. Just be quiet. Imagine that you have gone with Jesus and just the two of you have left the houseful of people and are together in a solitary place, just being quiet. Keep your expectations simple—you only want to spend time with Jesus, watching him pray. Listen to him. He's praying for you. He knows what you need and what he hopes for you, and you are simply sitting there, receiving the gift of being at his side.

Sabbath Reflection

Read this week's text out loud. Then read slowly through this reflection. It's up to you whether to include your family or others in this practice. If you do include children, depending on their ages, you can read this to them, summarize it, or simply ask them for their observations about the story. If you have a children's Bible, you could read the story from that version. Be open to the idea that they may have some insights that God can use to speak to you. You can use the questions

*at the end with others or on your own. Use as many or as few of the
questions as you like.*

Jesus was very popular. Later in his life, people would get pretty
mad at him, but for now, the Bible says, everyone was amazed.
They wanted to see him; they wanted to be around him.
Imagine that you are Jesus and everyone thinks you are amazing and wise. They want to be with you. What would you do?
How would you act? Do you think it would be tempting to believe
you really were "all that"?

Popularity can mess with you: get you believing what people
say about you, make you believe you're close to perfect, or at
least pretty special. Jesus *was* perfect, since he was God's Son. If
anyone had a right to feel proud and special, it was Jesus. But he
did not develop an attitude. Instead, he was humble.

How does he stay humble? Just by trying? Well, look at what
Jesus did—how he lived his ordinary life. In the synagogue and
at Peter's house, the Bible says, he healed people, and everyone
was amazed. But the next morning, what does he do? He goes
off to a "solitary place." He escapes from his admirers and claims
solitude. He shuts out their voices so he can listen to God.

If we want to be like Jesus, we can't do it just by trying really
hard. If we want to be like Jesus when we're in front of other
people, we have to behave like him behind the scenes. We'll need
to act like he did in private if we ever hope to be anything like
him in public. We will have to decide that his opinion is more
important than other people's opinions. Everyone thought Jesus
was great. He was popular. But that didn't matter to him. What
mattered was his Father's opinion—and he got away from the
crowds to be with God and be reminded that God, his heavenly
Father, loved him.

What did Jesus do when no one was looking, while everyone
else was still sleeping? He went off to pray, to talk to God and
listen to God. Not because he thought he was "supposed to"
pray. Not so he could tell everyone later on how well his "quiet

time" had gone that morning, in an effort to impress them with his personal piety. Rather, he went away from those he served to be with the one he really loved. He sincerely wanted to be with his Father. He knew that God loved him not because he could do miracles but because of their relationship. He had been giving, healing, teaching. Time with his Father was not another task on his to-do list. Rather, it replenished his soul. Through time alone with his Father he regained perspective. He listened to God's voice and received abundant and unconditional love. Solitude offered Jesus a chance to breathe deeper, to bask in his Father's love.

God loves us in that same way—not because of the things we do but because we're his children. And one way we can make sure we remember that is to live like Jesus did and take some time to pray, to listen, to simply be alone with God on a regular basis.

questions

What do you notice about Jesus in this passage? What is he like? How do you think he feels?

Imagine that you are a sick person who comes to Jesus at Simon Peter's house. How do you feel about meeting Jesus? What is it like to be healed? Describe what happens to you—use your imagination and pretend that you were healed and now you are telling others about it.

Why do you think Jesus got up early? Do you like to spend time by yourself? Why or why not?

Week Nine

Two Daughters

When Jesus went back across to the other side of the lake, a large crowd gathered around him on the shore. A leader of the local synagogue, whose name was Jairus, came and fell down before him, pleading with him to heal his little daughter. "She is about to die," he said in desperation. "Please come and place your hands on her; heal her so she can live."

Jesus went with him, and the crowd thronged behind. And there was a woman in the crowd who had had a hemorrhage for twelve years. She had suffered a great deal from many doctors through the years and had spent everything she had to pay them, but she had gotten no better. In fact, she was worse. She had heard about Jesus, so she came up behind him through the crowd and touched the fringe of his robe. For she thought to herself, "If I can just touch his clothing, I will be healed." Immediately the bleeding stopped, and she could feel that she had been healed!

Jesus realized at once that healing power had gone out from him, so he turned around in the crowd and asked, "Who touched my clothes?"

His disciples said to him, "All this crowd is pressing around you. How can you ask, 'Who touched me?'"

But he kept on looking around to see who had done it. Then the frightened woman, trembling at the realization of what had happened to her, came and fell at his feet and told him what she had done. And he said *to her, "Daughter, your faith has made you well. Go in peace. You have been healed."*

While he was still speaking to her, messengers arrived from Jairus's home with the message, "Your daughter is dead. There's no use troubling the Teacher now."

But Jesus ignored their comments and said to Jairus, "Don't be afraid. Just trust me." Then Jesus stopped the crowd and wouldn't let anyone go with him except Peter and James and John. When they came to the home of the synagogue leader, Jesus saw the commotion and the weeping and wailing. He went inside and spoke to the people. "Why all this weeping and commotion?" he asked. "The child isn't dead; she is only asleep."

The crowd laughed at him, but he told them all to go outside. Then he took the girl's father and mother and his three disciples into the room where the girl was lying. Holding her hand, he said to her, "Get up, little girl!" And the girl, who was twelve years old, immediately stood up and walked around! Her parents were absolutely overwhelmed. Jesus commanded them not to tell anyone what had happened, and he told them to give her something to eat.

Mark 5:21–43 NLT

Day One: Deep Listening

In this practice, remember, you are listening to God through his Word, the Bible. It is a method both of meditating on Scripture and of prayer, of hearing and then responding.

Take a few moments to settle yourself. Take a deep breath, and release any tension in your body. Ask God to simply meet you and speak to you through this passage. Especially with this particular passage, remember that he does not condemn you. Listen for the voice of love. If you hear the voice of shame, that is not God's voice.

Read through the passage slowly, out loud if possible. Listen for the word or phrase that stands out to you. After you read, spend several minutes in silence. Let the word that stood out echo in your mind.

Read slowly through the passage again, listening for the word, phrase, or thought that seems to resonate with you. Spend some time simply turning that word or phrase over in your mind. What does God want to say to you? Is there some encouragement or challenge from him in this word? What does he want you to know?

Spend as long as you need in silence, thinking about what God has said. When you are ready, read the passage one more time, listening again for God's word to you. Remember that he speaks with the voice of love. Is there something he wants you to do?

Reflect on what God has said to you through this passage. Let this time lead you into a dialogue with God or a comfortable silence, knowing that either way, you are in his presence and deeply loved.

End your time by thanking him for speaking with you through his Word. Write a sentence or two on your life card about what God has said to you.

Day Two: Breath Prayer

Read through the passage slowly, listening for God's voice. See if there is a word or phrase that you want to use as your prayer. If you like, try reading another version to look for words or phrases that resonate with you.

You may want to use Jesus's words to Jairus: "Don't be afraid; just trust me" (v. 36). Or you may want to turn some part of the woman's experience into your prayer: "I will be healed" (v. 28) or "freed from her suffering" (v. 29). Perhaps one of these gives a name to the deep desire of your heart, and you can use it to focus your listening prayer. Reflect for a moment: What are you afraid of? What do you need to be healed of? How could Jesus set you free? What blocks you from believing that Jesus's power can heal you?

Find a place where you can be still and quiet. Breathe slowly and deeply for a few minutes. Let go of distracting thoughts. If you need to, keep a sheet of paper nearby to jot down what seem like important things you need to remember. Set the paper aside when you are ready to be still. Trust Jesus to hold those things for you while you focus on him. Breathe in his presence. Use the prayer word or phrase to keep you focused when distractions come, but mostly, simply be still, relaxing in God's love.

Day Three: Kindness

Notice that Jesus is interrupted in this passage. He's teaching when Jairus comes up and interrupts, asking Jesus to come to his home and heal his daughter. Jesus agrees to go to the child, but on the way, he's interrupted again by the woman who has been subject to bleeding. But he sees these interruptions as opportunities to love. These people are not pulling him away from his task; they are his task. He came not to be served but to serve, and at each of these moments, he lives out that mission by giving his attention.

Today, be open to interruptions. Each time you are interrupted, trust that God is speaking through the interruption. Give love, attention, and practical assistance to the person who is interrupting you. Treat that person as if they were Jesus. Believe that those who ask for your attention really do need it and that God has assigned you the task of extending his love to that particular person.

Sabbath Reflection

Read the text out loud. Then read slowly through this reflection.
It's up to you whether to include your family or others in this practice.
If you do include children, depending on their ages, you can read
this to them, summarize it, or simply ask them for their observations
about the story. If you have a children's Bible, you could read the
story from that version. Be open to the idea that they may have some
insights that God can use to speak to you. You can use the questions
at the end with others or on your own. Use as many or as few of the
questions as you like.

Who do you look to as an example of faith? Perhaps a pastor or other teacher—someone who seems to be "religious" or "spiritual."

Whose spiritual life do you want to emulate? Maybe you know someone who seems to have it all together, who seems like she has no problems, thanks to the fact that Jesus has blessed her so.

In my experience, people who seem to have perfect lives rarely do. Two things can fool us into thinking someone has no problems: either we don't know them well enough, or they spend a lot of energy hiding what's really going on.

I think sometimes the best spiritual mentors are people whose struggles have given them a gritty, raw, but very real faith. People who have asked tough questions that ultimately strengthened their faith.

In this story, Jesus points to someone we might not expect as an example of faith. According to Jewish law, a woman having her period was considered "unclean." According to the Old Testament laws (see Lev. 15:25–30) a woman with an abnormal flow of blood was considered unclean, as was anything she lay on or sat on, or anyone who touched her bed or anything she'd sat on.

One commentary notes: "Her 'flow of blood' or 'hemorrhages' excluded her from normal social contact and religious or cultic activity. She has effectively been excluded from society for twelve years. . . . this woman takes the initiative to go to Jesus, ignoring the social custom that would have prevented her from speaking to a male in public and the cultic, blood taboos that would prevent physical contact."[1]

This woman was desperate, but bold. Her suffering did not defeat her, but filled her with an amazing faith. Men, especially rabbis, did not speak to women in public. If she touched Jesus, a rabbi, she would render him "unclean"—and that would get her into big trouble. Still, she risks it. Maybe she figures the risk is better than continuing to suffer alone anymore. But Jesus responds in a way that turns the law upside down—instead of her contaminating him, he "decontaminates" her by immediately healing her uncleanness.

As if this weren't surprising enough, he stops to talk with her, to offer not only physical healing but spiritual and emotional restoration as well. He welcomes her back to the family of faith with the words, "Daughter, your faith has made you well." Instead of pointing to her as a sinner, an unclean woman (the label she'd worn for twelve years), he now holds her up as an example, to the surprised crowd, and to Jairus.

But while he was doing that, Jairus's daughter died. Jairus was, of course, very upset. I can imagine him beginning to wail and cry—and to question. Why did Jesus stop to deal with this crazy woman? I think there was fear and grief on Jairus's face, because look at what Jesus says to him.

> "Don't be afraid; just have faith," he says to Jairus. And they both look at the woman, the one who should have been afraid but wasn't. The one kneeling on the ground thinking she'd be struck dead for her boldness, her chutzpah, and instead finding herself blessed beyond what she could ever hope or imagine. The one whose faith, Jesus had just proclaimed, had healed her. The one Jesus called "daughter." She's just as much a daughter as the child of an "important" man, just as loved. Jesus tells Jairus, through both words and actions: "Don't be afraid. Just have faith, like this

unclean woman, like this person you don't think even matters. Don't despise her. Aspire to be like her."[2]

Whom do you look to as a spiritual role model? Is it someone who seems to be successful or "blessed"? What about people who have suffered, or are still suffering, yet continue to believe, to trust that God is in control?

Be open today to the idea that God may want to use someone unexpected to be an example to you of what it means to live a life of faith. If you are going through a time of suffering, trust that Jesus sees you and wants to heal you. You are his beloved daughter. He may even want to use your life to inspire others to greater faith.

Don't be afraid; just believe.

questions

Who are your spiritual role models?

Is there an ongoing pain or issue in your life that you need Jesus to touch and heal?

How have seasons of pain and suffering in your own life affected your spiritual growth?

What is an area where you need to let go of fear and have faith?

Week Ten

"You Feed Them"

The apostles gathered around Jesus and reported to him all they had done and taught. Then, because so many people were coming and going that they did not even have a chance to eat, he said to them, "Come with me by yourselves to a quiet place and get some rest."

So they went away by themselves in a boat to a solitary place. But many who saw them leaving recognized them and ran on foot from all the towns and got there ahead of them. When Jesus landed and saw a large crowd, he had compassion on them, because they were like sheep without a shepherd. So he began teaching them many things.

By this time it was late in the day, so his disciples came to him. "This is a remote place," they said, "and it's already very late. Send the people away so that they can go to the surrounding countryside and villages and buy themselves something to eat."

But he answered, "You give them something to eat."

They said to him, "That would take almost a year's wages! Are we to go and spend that much on bread and give it to them to eat?"

"How many loaves do you have?" he asked. "Go and see."

When they found out, they said, "Five—and two fish."

Then Jesus directed them to have all the people sit down in groups on the green grass. So they sat down in groups of hundreds and fifties. Taking the five loaves and the two fish and looking up to heaven, he gave thanks and broke the loaves. Then he gave them to his disciples to set before the people. He also divided the two fish among them all. They all *ate and were satisfied, and the disciples picked up twelve basketfuls of broken pieces of bread and fish. The number of the men who had eaten was five thousand.*

Mark 6:30–44

Day One: Solitude

At the beginning of this passage, Jesus notices that his disciples have been busy—so busy they have not had time even to eat. So he says to them, "Come with me by yourselves to a quiet place and get some rest" (v. 31).

Today, take a moment to respond to that invitation. Solitude is simply time alone with Jesus. It's a chance to rest, to catch your breath. Perhaps you've had time to eat, but you haven't had time to feed your soul, and that's what solitude can do.

Plan ahead—find someone to watch your children, if you need to. Don't let other obligations interrupt your time. If someone asks, tell them you have an appointment—you don't have to explain any further. Get out of the house; turn off your cell phone.

When you go to be alone, to come away with Jesus and get some rest, bring as little as possible. Make this a time of self-examination: Are you so busy that you don't have time to care for yourself, either physically or spiritually? What do you sense Jesus is saying to you about how you are caring for your body and soul?

Don't bring lots of books and study materials—perhaps you'll want only a couple of the life cards that you've collected over the last few weeks. Pick two or three that have significant insights written on them, and use your time of solitude to reflect on these. Take something small and allow it to nourish you spiritually.

Day Two: Being There

Read through this week's Scripture passage. What do you notice about Jesus? How would you describe him based on this passage?

Imagine yourself in the scene, perhaps as one of the disciples: You've been working hard and looking forward to spending some time alone with Jesus, perhaps enjoying a simple meal with just him and the other disciples. And suddenly the crowds are there again.

Or imagine you are a part of the crowd—hungry to be with Jesus, at first, but eventually physically hungry as well. Imagine eating that miraculous meal. What do the fish and bread taste like? What do you think as you chew it? What are the people around you saying as they pass out the food? What is the conversation about—are you discussing what Jesus taught all day, or are you in awe of the miracle? In a crowd of five thousand men (plus women and children who probably weren't included in the count but certainly got to eat), are you even aware of how little there was to start with? How about when the leftovers are gathered up? What do you see and smell?

Take five or ten minutes to simply imagine the scene from several different perspectives.

Think for a moment about Jesus. Read the passage and give him your attention. How do you think he is feeling? What do you imagine he is thinking?

What do you love about Jesus as you watch this scene? What confuses you or rubs you the wrong way? Imagine you are a disciple and Jesus tells you to feed the crowd. What do you think, feel, say?

By imagining yourself in the scene, you are spending time with Jesus. Don't rush to talk it over with him, but simply observe for a while. Daydream about the scene, mulling slowly over the details.

Bring any questions or thankfulness you have to him in prayer. Simply sit with whatever comes to you for a few moments. Don't rush.

Add one sentence to your life card about what you noticed about Jesus or what he said to you as you imagined yourself in the scene.

Day Three: Kindness

Read through the passage slowly. Ask God to show you how you might share his love with others. Jesus asked his disciples to give very practical help to the crowd. What sort of practical help might he be asking you to give to someone?

Notice that Jesus does not say to his disciples, "Don't worry, I'll feed them." Rather, he says, "You give them something to eat" (v. 37).

Take that phrase as God's word to you today. Listen carefully to it. Whom does he want you to feed? Is he asking you to feed that person physically (say by preparing a meal for them or dropping off a bag of groceries) or spiritually (perhaps by writing them an encouraging note or taking them out for coffee just to listen to them)?

Pray for the courage to do what he is asking you to do.

Sabbath Reflection

Read the text out loud. Then read slowly through this reflection. It's up to you whether to include your family or others in this practice. If you do include children, depending on their ages, you can read this to them, summarize it, or simply ask them for their observations about the story.

If you have a children's Bible, you could read the story from that version. Be open to the idea that they may have some insights that God can use to speak to you. You can use the questions at the end with others or on your own. Use as many or as few of the questions as you like.

At the beginning of this passage, we learn that Jesus and his disciples have been busy. Too busy to even eat.

The disciples came to Jesus, telling him how they had ministered to others. They had been sent out to teach and heal, and having done that, they returned to tell Jesus about it.

And Jesus celebrates their success, but then he says, "Okay, don't get too wrapped up in the accolades of the crowd. Come away with me. It is time to rest."

They agree, but people follow. And Jesus's compassion for his disciples extends to the crowds. He begins to teach them.

I imagine the disciples might be a little unhappy with this. They thought they were going to have some time alone with Jesus and perhaps enjoy a meal together. After all, the text says they didn't have time to eat. Then suddenly the crowd is there again, demanding Jesus's attention.

As he often does, Jesus sees the interruption as an opportunity to love, to do what he has been called to do: announce the arrival of God's kingdom. And he knows it will also be an opportunity to teach his disciples even more about trust.

I'm thinking those disciples were a little hungry and tired and as a result getting a bit cranky. Did they even listen to whatever it was that Jesus was teaching? They are the first to say, "Isn't it time for dinner yet?" They tell Jesus, "Send these people away. Tell them to go get themselves something to eat. We're hungry, and maybe they are too."

I think the disciples were hoping to get dinner as well. They wanted Jesus to fix the problem. "You do it, Jesus. Send them away. And while you're at it, can we have some dinner?"

Jesus tells them, *"You* give them something to eat." You can do it, he's telling them. Even when you are hungry and tired. They object, of course. Impossible. This is a team that just returned from teaching and doing miracles in Jesus's name, but they can't imagine feeding this huge crowd.

Jesus says, "Start with what you've got."

In this case, it wasn't much. But he had the disciples organize the people to sit in big groups. And he said, "Feed them." Was it Jesus's prayer of thanks, his hand on the meager portions, that turned it into abundance? Was it the disciples' obedience in the face of a ridiculous situation?

Miraculously, there was more than enough. There were even twelve baskets of leftovers, which the text notes that the disciples gathered. I'm guessing those hungry disciples ate some of that meal. What was that like for them, to swallow their doubts?

What did that meal do for them? Besides filling their bellies, I think it nourished their souls. It was a reminder that when we feed others, we ourselves are fed.

When we are tired and hungry and feel we have nothing to give, Jesus will sometimes still call us to feed others, to serve them, to give them what we think we don't even have. To start with what we've got, which may not be much. But the little we have is enough. And in feeding others, we ourselves are nourished, strengthened, sustained.

questions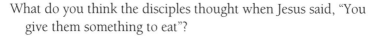

What do you think the disciples thought when Jesus said, "You give them something to eat"?

Tell about a time when you had to give to others although you felt depleted. How were you able to do it?

Have you ever been "fed" spiritually by "feeding" others? Describe what happened.

85

Week Eleven Mark 10:17–27

He Went Away Sad

As Jesus started on his way, a man ran up to him and fell on his knees before him. "Good teacher," he asked, "what must I do to inherit eternal life?"

"Why do you call me good?" Jesus answered. "No one is good—except God alone. You know the commandments: 'You shall not murder, you shall not commit adultery, you shall not steal, you shall not give false testimony, you shall not defraud, honor your father and mother.'"

"Teacher," he declared, "all these I have kept since I was a boy."

Jesus looked at him and loved him. "One thing you lack," he said. "Go, sell everything you have and give to the poor, and you will have treasure in heaven. Then come, follow me."

At this the man's face fell. He went away sad, because he had great wealth.

Jesus looked around and said to his disciples, "How hard it is for the rich to enter the kingdom of God!"

The disciples were amazed at his words. But Jesus said again, "Children, how hard it is to enter the kingdom of God! It is easier for a camel to go through the eye of a needle than for the rich to enter the kingdom of God."

The disciples were even more amazed, and said to each other, "Who then can be saved?"

Jesus looked at them and said, "With human beings this is impossible, but not with God; all things are possible with God."

Mark 10:17–27

Day One: Deep Listening

In this practice, remember, you are listening to God through his Word, the Bible. It is a method both of meditating on Scripture and of prayer, of hearing and then responding.

Take your time; settle your body, your soul. Breathe deeply, and release any tension. Ask God to simply meet you and speak to you through his Word. Come to this practice expectant, ready to hear from Jesus.

Read through the passage slowly, out loud if possible. Listen for the word or phrase that stands out to you. After you read, spend several minutes in silence. Let the word that stood out echo in your mind.

Read slowly through the passage again, listening for the word, phrase, or thought that seems to resonate with you. Spend some time simply turning that word or phrase over in your mind. What does God want to say to you? Is there some encouragement or challenge from him in this word? What does he want you to know?

Spend as long as you need in silence, thinking about what God has said. When you are ready, read the passage one more time, listening again for God's word to you. Remember that he speaks with the voice of love. Is there something he wants you to do?

Reflect on what God has said to you through this passage. Let this time lead you into a dialogue with God or a comfortable silence, knowing that either way, you are in his presence and deeply loved.

End your time by thanking him for speaking with you through his Word. Write a phrase or two on your life card about what God has said to you.

Day Two: Journaling

Jesus tells his disciples in this passage, "How hard it is for the rich to enter the kingdom of God!" (v. 23).

Spend some time journaling about your gut response to this question. Then use the following questions to guide your journaling time.

Do you think of yourself as rich? If you have a roof overhead and food to eat, you are richer than most of the people in the world. If we never interact with the truly poor, how will that affect our ability to accurately assess our own relative wealth?

What does it mean to "enter the kingdom of God"? Do you think Jesus is talking about going to heaven after we die? Consider the fact that Jesus kept telling people, "the kingdom of God is at hand," and "the kingdom of God is among you." Could Jesus be talking about life right now, in this world? What makes it hard for someone who is focused on their financial portfolio to participate in God's kingdom in this world?

How might giving money to the poor help us to participate more fully in what God is doing right now?

Day Three: Breath Prayer

Set aside some time to be quiet. You may need to get out of the house. Find a place where you can be still and quiet.

Breathe slowly and deeply for a few minutes. Let go of distracting thoughts.

Read through the passage slowly, noticing how it makes you feel. Does a certain phrase or sentence create an emotional response? Do you feel comforted or uncomfortable? Challenged or reassured? Sad or happy?

Can you turn that response into a simple prayer, one you can say in the space of a single breath?

What do you need from Jesus? Simply sit with your response to the passage for a few moments, and let a single-sentence prayer come from deep in your heart. Jesus loved this man in spite of his spiritual blindness. Perhaps you will want to pray, "Jesus, love me." What do you need?

Sit quietly, knowing that Jesus is as close as the air you breathe. When you find yourself getting distracted, use your breath prayer to bring yourself gently back into an awareness of his loving presence.

Sabbath Reflection

Read the text out loud. Then read slowly through this reflection. It's up to you whether to include your family or others in this practice. If you do include children, depending on their ages, you can read this to them, summarize it, or simply ask them for their observations about the story. If you have a children's Bible, you could read the story from that version. Be open to the idea that they may have some insights that God can use to speak to you. You can use the questions at the end with others or on your own. Use as many or as few of the questions as you like.

Just before he's approached by this young man, Jesus had a group of children on his lap. He'd just used them to illustrate a great truth: Childlike faith and trust is not only a good idea but necessary if we are to enter the kingdom. Our own accomplishments will not do it.

Children in Jesus's day lived humbly. They were not soccer stars by the time they were five, nor did they assume that the world revolved around them. They quickly learned that was not the case. Their parents loved them, sure, but most children at that time knew what it meant to work hard, serving their family in the home, working the fields, herding sheep.

As Jesus leaves the children, this wealthy young man hurries up. The text says he "ran up to him" (v. 17). Was he enthusiastic or just in a hurry? Can't you picture him striding over to Jesus? If he lived today, he might be busy checking on his investments on his cell phone while hurrying toward Jesus. "I've got people to see, places to be, but I need to get some info—how can I inherit eternal life?"

He's already inherited a lot, most likely—maybe some investments, a vacation home on the Sea of Galilee, and a condo in Jerusalem. He also thinks he's got his balance sheet in order spiritually—he's kept all the rules, or thinks he has. He wants to make sure he's got this nailed down too.

Jesus doesn't tell him, "To inherit eternal life you need to keep the commandments." He says, "No one is good—except God alone" (v. 18). His point is to say, "Okay, you just called me 'good'—does that mean you believe I'm God? Or just a 'good teacher'? Do you even know what you're saying?"

I think Jesus is also pointing out to him, "You think it's about 'being good,' but it's not. It's about humility." Don't you wonder if this young man saw Jesus interacting with the children just moments before? Jesus is trying to tell him that accomplishments, whether they are in the business or financial realm or in keeping the religious rules, don't help. No one is good.

Then Jesus says, "You know the commandments" (v. 19). He's not saying that they are the way to eternal life either. He's just stating a fact: "You know those commandments, right?" I don't know, but I wonder if he was going to say, "You know those commandments? They are not really going to be enough to get you eternal life either," except that the man interrupts to say that he's basically never sinned.

Think of the chutzpah, the nerve. He's called Jesus good, and Jesus says, "Oh, really? Do you believe you're having a conversation with God? And if you do, you have the nerve to say you've never broken a commandment, including that one about 'false testimony'—that is, lying? Really?"

Jesus knows this guy has his priorities totally screwed up. He's moving too fast; he's not even really paying attention to the conversation he's having. He just wants an insurance policy. He wants to cross "eternal life" off his shopping list.

Amazingly, Jesus does not get annoyed. He sees right through this wealthy young man. He's rude, he's a liar, he's flippantly sycophantic, calling Jesus "good teacher." He's pretty sure he can buy his way into heaven somehow.

What just floors me about Jesus in this story is verse 21: "Jesus looked at him and loved him."

Really? He loved him?

I am not always humble when I come to Jesus. I am sometimes hurried, sometimes taking his attention for granted. I'm not proud of it, but I can act like this young man. I can be a jerk in my interactions with Jesus sometimes.

When I am this way, I sometimes think that Jesus will be annoyed with me or angry. He will sigh, roll his eyes, shake his head. Love me less, somehow.

The amazing truth is that we all come to Jesus, at least once in a while, like this young man. Selfish, hurried, deluded about our strengths, blind to our shortcomings.

And Jesus looks at us and loves us. Loves us.

Later Jesus says, "All things are possible with God" (v. 7).

The impossible thing that God makes possible is that we, in our sin, in our self-absorption, could be loved like that.

questions

What do you think this young man really wanted? Why do you think he went away sad?

When you think of "security," what do you think of? If Jesus were to tell you to sell all you had and give the money to the poor, would you feel secure?

In what ways is this wealthy man spiritually poor? What do you have in common with him?

Week Twelve Mark 12:28–34

The Greatest Command

One of the teachers of the law came and heard them debating. Noticing that Jesus had given them a good answer, he asked him, "Of all the commandments, which is the most important?"

"The most important one," answered Jesus, "is this: 'Hear, O Israel: The Lord our God, the Lord is one. Love the Lord your God with all your heart and with all your soul and with all your mind and with all your strength.' The second is this: 'Love your neighbor as yourself.' There is no commandment greater than these."

"Well said, teacher," the man replied. "You are right in saying that God is one and there is no other but him. To love him with all your heart, with all your understanding and with all your strength, and to love your neighbor as yourself is more important than all burnt offerings and sacrifices."

When Jesus saw that he had answered wisely, he said to him, "You are not far from the kingdom of God." And from then on no one dared ask him any more questions.

Mark 12:28–34

Week Twelve

Day One: Kindness

In this passage Jesus states that the most important command-ment is to love God and love other people. Jesus links these two key tenets of the Jewish faith together in a new way. Loving others is a way to express our love to God.

Who do you know who seems to have a shortage of love in their life? Maybe they are cranky or difficult to get along with. Maybe they are going through a difficult season. It is hard for us sometimes to approach someone who does not seem very loving. But it is precisely this person, the one who has a "love shortage," who needs our sisterly love the most. The person seemingly devoid of Jesus's love is the one who needs us to be Jesus to them.

What can you do today to show loving-kindness to someone who needs it desperately? Write a note, make a phone call? Leave flowers anonymously on their doorstep? Offer to buy them a cup of coffee and just listen to them for a while?

Ask God to direct you, then pray for the courage to obey as you share his love with someone who really needs it.

Day Two: Being There

You may want to read the entire chapter of Matthew 12 to get the context of the conversation Jesus has with the scribe in verses 28–34.

Read the passage and try to imagine the scene. In Jesus's time, philosophers and religious leaders loved to gather to discuss and debate. We do this today, but thanks to modern technology, the forum for this type of thing is usually talk radio or Internet blogs.

The earlier verses say that the various religious leaders came to Jesus. Where do you think he was? Jesus often taught out in

94

the countryside, but in this case, Mark 11:27 tells us, he was in Jerusalem. The religious leaders, it might seem, had the home court advantage.

Imagine you are in the crowd, watching Jesus interact with the religious leaders. What do you notice about him? What is he like? How do people respond to him? Is there a crowd watching him debate with the various groups of religious leaders? Is anyone getting angry and shouting? Or is the discussion calm and cool? Is there underlying tension?

Imagine yourself as the scribe, boldly asking Jesus a question, then responding to him. What does it feel like to be told, "You are not far from the kingdom of God" (v. 34)?

Day Three: Solitude

What does it mean to love God with all your heart, soul, mind, and strength? Think about the person you love most on this earth: perhaps your spouse, your child, your sister, or a parent. How do you let them know you love them?

A love relationship grows deeper when we spend time with our beloved. While we may enjoy spending time with that person along with others, we also desire at times to have time that is exclusive—just the two of us.

Solitude is simply time alone with God—it is a way of loving him.

Set aside some time today to simply be with God. Express your love to him creatively: perhaps by drawing, writing a poem or story, singing to him, even through your body by dancing or moving. Put on a worship CD and sing and dance to God. Let go of fear—whatever you share with him, however you choose to express your love, he will be delighted.

Sabbath Reflection

Read the text out loud. Then read slowly through this reflection. It's up to you whether to include your family or others in this practice. If you do include children, depending on their ages, you can read this to them, summarize it, or simply ask them for their observations about the story. If you have a children's Bible, you could read the story from that version. Be open to the idea that they may have some insights that God can use to speak to you. You can use the questions at the end with others or on your own. Use as many or as few of the questions as you like.

In Jesus's time, faithful Jews made it a part of their spiritual practice to recite the Shema, or creed of Israel, twice a day. When they gathered in the synagogue, they would recite it together: "Hear, O Israel: The LORD our God, the LORD is one" (Deut. 6:4).

I have a Jewish friend who tells me that when she goes to a Shabbat service at her temple, the congregation says the Shema together. She says it's a beautiful practice, reminding her of her heritage, connecting her with her faith, with her community, and with God. Even the word *Shema*, when you say it slowly, has a restful sound: *shhh . . . ummmm . . . ahhhh.*

This text tells us a "teacher of the law" or a "scribe" has been listening to Jesus talking with the religious leaders. He's impressed with Jesus. The scribes were a group of religious leaders who originally had served, as their name implies, to simply transcribe the law. "Gradually the scribes took on the responsibility of also interpreting and teaching the law; by New Testament times they had developed into a class of professionals who were devoted to the law's preservation and exposition."[1]

So here was a person who was dedicated to understanding God's Word and taught it to other people. This man probably would have had the whole Torah, the first five books of the Old Testament, memorized. He knew the ins and outs not only of the Scriptures but also of the oral traditions, which were the laws religious leaders had added, by way of interpretation, to the scriptural law.

Why does someone who would be considered an expert ask Jesus, "What do you think is the most important thing in the law?"

Jesus says, "It's the basics. You know that creed you recite twice a day? Start living it out. You can do so by loving others."

The man agrees; he affirms what Jesus says. And Jesus tells him, "You are not far from the kingdom of God" (v. 34). Does he mean, "not quite, but you've almost got it"? If so, what is the scribe missing?

I have studied the Bible; I teach it to others. I write about it; I write about Christian spirituality, about living the Christian life. I don't pretend to be an expert, but I am a student. This scribe and I, perhaps we walk on common ground. So what can I learn from him, one scribe to another?

Here's what I think this man walked away with: it's great to be able to teach truth, but it's another thing altogether to be able to live out the truths you teach. As a writer, I teach people through my books, just as this scribe taught, debated, and discussed truth. I think Jesus challenged him to live out the "love God, love others" thing, rather than just tell people that it's a good idea.

I sense that Jesus is calling each of us to live out what we say we think is true rather than to debate the meaning or relative importance of various truths. To move beyond saying what are important doctrines for me to believe. And to move on to pondering and then acting upon questions like: What is God's heart toward me? How will I respond to that? How can I develop compassion?

The most important thing is not knowledge *about* God but relationship *with* God. Love God with all you've got. Don't just recite a creed or give the right answers. Live them out. How? By sharing that amazing, all-encompassing love with others.

questions

What does it mean to love God with all your heart, soul, mind, and strength?

What keeps you from loving God in this way—perhaps a habit or possession in your life that blocks your ability to love God?

What do you notice about Jesus in this passage? What draws you toward him? What makes you uncomfortable or raises questions? What are those questions?

Week Thirteen Mark 12:41–44

Sacrificial Giving

Sitting across from the offering box, he was observing how the crowd tossed money in for the collection. Many of the rich were making large contributions. One poor widow came up and put in two small coins—a measly two cents. Jesus called his disciples over and said, "The truth is that this poor widow gave more to the collection than all the others put together. All the others gave what they'll never miss; she gave extravagantly what she couldn't afford—she gave her all."

Mark 12:41–44 Message

Day One: Journaling

Jesus commends the widow for giving "what she couldn't afford." Why do you think Jesus applauds her behavior? Journal about your experiences with giving.

Write about the following questions: Do you make it a practice to give? Does giving bring you joy, or does it frighten you? Do you think of yourself as wealthy or poor? How does this affect your giving?

Day Two: Deep Listening

Deep listening is a way to converse with God that allows him to speak first. By meditating on his Word, we listen to him, and it takes us to a deeper kind of prayer, a kind of listening in which we let go of controlling the conversation and let God truly say what he wants, not what we want. Hearing him, we respond with praise.

In this practice, the goal is simply to hear God and respond to him.

Take a few deep breaths. Allow yourself to slow down, both physically and mentally. Release any tension in your body. Ask God to simply meet you and speak to you through this passage.

Read through the passage slowly, out loud if possible. Listen for the word or phrase that stands out to you. After you read, spend several minutes in silence. Let the word that stood out echo in your mind.

Read slowly through the passage again, listening for the word, phrase, or thought that seems to resonate with you. Spend some time simply turning that word or phrase over in your mind. What does God want to say to you? Is there some encourage-ment or challenge from him in this word? What does he want you to know?

Spend as long as you need in silence, thinking about what God has said, chewing, as it were, on the bread of his word. When you are ready, read the passage one more time, listening again for God's word to you. Remember that he speaks with the voice of love. Is there something he wants you to do?

Reflect on what God has said to you through this passage. Let this time lead you into a dialogue with God, into communication with him, or to a deeper place of silent communion with him. Don't try to force anything: Remember that even if you are not aware of it, you are in his presence and deeply loved.

End your time by thanking him for speaking with you through his Word. Write a sentence or two on your life card about what God has asked you to do or be. Carry the card with you, reading it occasionally as a reminder to live out his love for you.

Day Three: Kindness

This week, look for opportunities to give. Ask God to show you some needs other than your own, and have the courage to obey when he says, "Give."

Right now things are a bit tight for our family financially, even though my husband and I are working. But I have a couple of neighbors who are unemployed. Things are much more difficult for them than they are for me. When I ask them if I can help, they say, "Just pray." So I pray. As I do, God reminds me that prayer is not just talking. It's listening, noticing where he's at work, and joining him in that work. Prayer is completed by action, by obedience. And God says, "You think you're poor, but you're not." He calls me to give.

What kindness can you show this week? Even if you feel you are poor and have only a little for yourself, how can you give (time, money, things) generously?

Sabbath Reflection

Read the text out loud. Then read slowly through this reflection. It's up to you whether to include your family or others in this practice.

If you do include children, depending on their ages, you can read this to them, summarize it, or simply ask them for their observations about the story. If you have a children's Bible, you could read the story from that version. Be open to the idea that they may have some insights that God can use to speak to you. You can use the questions at the end with others or on your own. Use as many or as few of the questions as you like.

This passage begins with Jesus sitting in the temple. Several versions say, "Jesus sat down" (v. 41). When a rabbi sat down in the temple, it meant he was getting ready to teach. In the passages just preceding this one, Jesus had already been teaching. Now he moves over near the place where the offerings were collected. The crowd was likely expecting some teaching from him.

I wonder what they expected to hear. Perhaps they thought he would praise the wealthy people. Maybe the wealthy people came up just at that time to showily drop their sacks of money into the collection basket in sight of Jesus. I don't know, but I imagine Jesus watching them and them smiling smugly at him as they deposit their offerings.

So Jesus watches and doesn't say anything at first. Then an unobtrusive widow quietly approaches and slides two small coins, together worth less than a penny, into the collection. She's embarrassed. She does not look at Jesus but keeps her head down. In that society, a widow had no rights, no one to take care of her, no means. She was at the bottom of the socioeconomic ladder. Her self-worth may have been as small as her offering.

But Jesus calls his disciples over. The object lesson has been shown, and now he will teach them. "The widow put in more than anyone," he says. What?

If the poor widow were around today, we would perhaps urge her to apply for food stamps and budget carefully, rather than commend her for giving away her last dime.

Jesus says the widow put in more than anyone else. God's economy is so odd, isn't it? Why does Jesus say she gave more? I think it's not just about numbers. It's about trust.

I often am tempted to wish I had more money so I could be more generous. But typically, the more you have, the harder it is to give it away. The rich people in this story gave a lot, but they didn't give sacrificially. They gave some of their excess. Their giving may have helped the temple, but it also built the house of their pride. To give a bit of your excess doesn't build your faith.

To give sacrificially means to give away more than you think you can. There is not a number or even a percentage of your income where you can say, "Okay, here's where sacrifice begins."

That's because giving is not about numbers. It's about your heart. What Jesus commends in this woman is what he calls each of us to: giving him all of ourselves. All of our trust. It's all his anyway. He gives us the ability to earn; he gives us life and breath. He provides and asks us to trust him by surrendering our whole self, including our finances, to him.

Sometimes we're called to give sacrificially of our time. Like just now, when my phone rang, interrupting my writing time, which seems limited these days anyway. It was my husband, asking me to come and pick him up (right now) at the car dealer, where his car is being repaired. And can he have my car until his is fixed? As I begin to protest—"I can't come get you, I'm busy writing about sacrificial giving"—the irony of it hits me. I stop and remind myself to just listen. To pry the small coins of my precious time from my clenched fist.

I breathe and ask Jesus for help. Scot and I discuss what would be the best way to handle having one car for part of the day and how to get both of us to the places we need to go. I speak carefully, trying to stay open to helping him, trying to be willing to give of my time. I wish I could give sacrificially, but right now, anything feels like a sacrifice. Then Scot offers to try to get someone from his office to pick him up now. I offer to pick him up later to get him to an appointment. We both give, and in that, we both receive.

I feel like Jesus just "sat down" next to me at my desk, watching me talk on the phone with my husband.

? ——————— questions

What would it mean for you to give sacrificially, either of your time or your money?

Do you make it a habit to give some of your money away? How has this affected you spiritually? If you think it hasn't affected you spiritually, consider the possibility that you may be missing out on something.

Do you feel you have an abundance of time or not enough? What happens when someone asks you to give them some of your time? What makes it hard to do that?

Week Fourteen Mark 14:32-42

Alone in the Garden

They went to a place called Gethsemane, and Jesus said to his disciples, "Sit here while I pray." He took Peter, James and John along with him, and he began to be deeply distressed and troubled. "My soul is overwhelmed with sorrow to the point of death," he said to them. "Stay here and keep watch."

Going a little farther, he fell to the ground and prayed that if possible the hour might pass from him. "Abba, Father," he said, "everything is possible for you. Take this cup from me. Yet not what I will, but what you will."

Then he returned to his disciples and found them sleeping. "Simon," he said to Peter, "are you asleep? Could you not keep watch for one hour? Watch and pray so that you will not fall into temptation. The spirit is willing, but the flesh is weak."

Once more he went away and prayed the same thing. When he came back, he again found them sleeping, because their eyes were heavy. They did not know what to say to him.

Returning the third time, he said to them, "Are you still sleeping and resting? Enough! The hour has come. Look, the Son of Man is delivered into the hands of sinners. Rise! Let us go! Here comes my betrayer!"

Mark 14:32–42

Day One: Breath Prayer

Set aside some time to be quiet. You may need to get out of the house. Find a place where you can be still and quiet. Breathe slowly and deeply for a few minutes. Let go of distracting thoughts.

Read through the passage slowly, noticing how it makes you feel. Does a certain phrase or sentence create an emotional response? Do you feel comforted or uncomfortable? Challenged or reassured? Sad or happy?

In this story, Jesus asked his disciples to simply be with him. They found this difficult. A breath prayer is a way to focus on Jesus, to simply be with him. Today Jesus asks the same of you: "Watch and pray. Just be with me." Remember that Jesus longs to be with you even more than you long to be with him.

Is there anything you feel troubled or distressed about? Jesus understands; he's experienced those feelings.

Simply sit with your response to the passage for a few moments, and let a single-sentence prayer, one you can say in the space of a single breath, come from deep in your heart. Spend time just being with Jesus, using your breath prayer to bring your attention back to him should you become distracted or tired.

Day Two: Being There

Read the passage slowly, imagining what it was like to be there. Put yourself in the place of one of the disciples, perhaps Peter or John. How do you feel? How do you respond to Jesus's intense sorrow? Do you feel sad? Overwhelmed? How do you feel when he rouses you sadly from sleep?

Use your senses to reconstruct the scene in your imagination. Perhaps you hear a dove cooing, punctuating the heavy evening.

Feel yourself sitting on the damp ground in a garden; smell the olive trees and flowers. Peer through the darkness, listen to Jesus's desperate prayers, feel the heaviness in your eyes as you fight the urge to just escape by falling asleep.

What do you notice about Jesus? So many other times he's seemed so confident and strong—here he seems perhaps weak, afraid, weary. What response do his emotions evoke in you?

After you've spent some time using your own imagination to reflect on this passage, you may want to rent a copy of the movie *The Passion of the Christ* and watch the opening scene. How does that film's depiction of Gethsemane differ from your own thoughts about it?

Day Three: Solitude

Throughout the Gospels, we read about Jesus retreating into solitude—going up on a mountain to pray, slipping away to a lonely place early in the morning. But in this moment, his darkest time, he asks friends to go with him to pray. He asks his disciples to pray with him, to support him, to be there.

They fail. No two ways about it. The disciples are there physically, but he is still alone. They seem unable to pray or even to stay awake. It had to be painful for him—especially because he knew that this was only the beginning. They'd abandon him completely, pretty soon.

When we need people and they let us down, we are forced into a solitude that we might not choose. But God is in that solitude. He does not abandon us. Jesus was not utterly alone. He remained in intimate conversation with his Abba, his loving Father. Though the disciples let him down, his Father did not.

Create some space to be alone with God today. Allow yourself to feel lonely, if that is what comes. Know that Jesus felt lonely too. In his loneliness he turned to his loving Father, knowing he was deeply loved, and surrendered to that love.

Follow Jesus to that lonely place and from there into the deep love of the Father.

Sabbath Reflection

Read the text out loud. Then read slowly through this reflection. It's up to you whether to include your family or others in this practice. If you do include children, depending on their ages, you can read this to them, summarize it, or simply ask them for their observations about the story. If you have a children's Bible, you could read the story from that version. Be open to the idea that they may have some insights that God can use to speak to you. You can use the questions at the end with others or on your own. Use as many or as few of the questions as you like.

"Take this cup from me."

Sometimes life feels like your own private Gethsemane. You feel pain; you feel alone, misunderstood. You wish it would be taken away. You ask others to pray, and they say they will, but you wonder—will they really? It's hard, even for you, to pray.

I have often prayed my own version of a Gethsemane prayer: *Abba, Father, everything is possible for you. Take this cup from me.* End of prayer. I don't want to add that crucial line that marks Jesus's entire life and ministry: *Yet not what I will, but what you will.*

Really?

Jesus faced a painful death—but others before him and many after him suffered a similar fate, at least from a physical standpoint. Certainly he was scared and anxious about dying a painful death. Still, the cup of suffering that Jesus did not want to drink was much more horrible than physical torture and death. It was something no one before or since has suffered, because no one but Jesus was perfectly sinless and made to take the punishment for all the sin of every person. No one else has experienced the intimacy with God that sinlessness affords. His perfect union with his heavenly Father would be broken—and the thought of that was what overwhelmed him. He took on himself the weight of the sins of mankind and God's wrath against them.

When Jesus returns to the disciples and finds them asleep, it's not just their lack of support that disturbs him. He's agonizing over the fact that he has to die not just for a faceless human race but more specifically for these sleepy disciples, the people he's loved, taught, and lived with for three years. He told them earlier that he would die for them, but they would fall away. They said they wouldn't leave, wouldn't deny him. But an hour later, they don't even seem to care.

Jesus is praying but perhaps also asking himself, Is it worth it, dying for people, taking their punishment? It would be easier, surely, if they were grateful, if it seemed like they understood the magnitude of this sacrifice and the pain—the enormity of what Jesus was doing for them. But they don't seem to. Jesus is pouring his heart out in prayer, and they fall asleep.

I think Jesus felt about as lonely as anyone ever could at that moment.

I wonder if he questioned the task before him. Why did he go back to the disciples repeatedly? Was he looking for reassurance that his sacrifice was worth it, that his mission somehow really *mattered*? If so, how did he feel coming back and finding his closest friends snoozing?

Jesus does not ask them to pray for him at first. He only asks that they "sit here while I pray" (v. 32). Jesus prays, and all they have to do is "keep watch" (v. 34).

When he finds them sleeping, he tells them to pray not for him but for themselves, that they would not be tempted to fall asleep, to zone out. Satan, I think, wants to convince Jesus that he ought not to drink the cup. He tempts Jesus to doubt: Why die for a bunch of ingrates who can't even sit and watch you pray, let alone pray themselves? What's the point of this? It is *so* not worth it.

But Jesus is stronger than Satan. Here's where the battle for your soul and mine is won—when Jesus decides that even if his disciples don't get it, he's going to move forward, believing that someday, they will. He's going to give us a priceless gift, even if we don't appreciate it.

When I am in pain or facing difficulties, I sometimes don't know how to pray. But Jesus does. And if I invite him, Jesus will come into my Gethsemane. He does so, not just because I need him to, but because he is willing to. He died so that we could live in relationship. His suffering allows me the privilege of intimacy with him, through both joys and sorrows. And his words to me are the words he said to his sleepy, fallible disciples: Sit here while I pray. Just be with me, and I'll pray for you.

We are not alone when we pray, tossing words at the ceiling and hoping we break through. Jesus not only comes to us, but *he prays for us*. The Bible says, "The Spirit helps us in our weakness. We do not know what we ought to pray for, but the Spirit himself intercedes for us with groans that words cannot express. And he who searches our hearts knows the mind of the Spirit, because the Spirit intercedes for the saints in accordance with God's will" (Rom. 8:26–27 NIV).

Jesus says, "Just watch while I pray." The Spirit intercedes for us "in accordance with God's will" (Rom. 8:27 NIV), which is what Jesus prayed with that crucial last line, "not what I will, but what you will" (Mark 14:36). Letting Jesus pray for us changes everything. We can let go of telling God precisely how he ought to remove our challenges and take away the cup of our suffering. We can focus instead on just being in the presence of Jesus, who tells us to simply watch him, to be awake and aware of him, and to listen while he prays for us in ways that are too deep for words. When we can't say "not my will but yours," Jesus says it for us. That is the gift of Gethsemane.

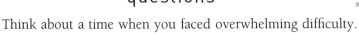

questions

Think about a time when you faced overwhelming difficulty. How did you pray? What happened in that situation?

Tell about a time someone else prayed for you. What was that like?

What do you think the Bible means when it says the Spirit prays for us?

What specific steps would help you to focus on being in Jesus's presence when you pray?

Week Fifteen

Visible Faith

One day Jesus was teaching, and Pharisees and teachers of the law were sitting there. They had come from every village of Galilee and from Judea and Jerusalem. And the power of the Lord was with Jesus to heal the sick. Some men came carrying a paralyzed man on a mat and tried to take him into the house to lay him before Jesus. When they could not find a way to do this because of the crowd, they went up on the roof and lowered him on his mat through the tiles into the middle of the crowd, right in front of Jesus.

When Jesus saw their faith, he said, "Friend, your sins are forgiven."

The Pharisees and the teachers of the law began thinking to themselves, "Who is this fellow who speaks blasphemy? Who can forgive sins but God alone?"

Jesus knew what they were thinking and asked, "Why are you thinking these things in your hearts? Which is easier: to say, 'Your sins are forgiven,' or to say, 'Get up and walk'? But I want you to know that the Son of Man has authority on earth to forgive sins." So he said to the paralyzed man, "I tell you, get up, take your mat and go home." Immediately he stood up in front of them, took what he had been lying on and went home praising God. Everyone was amazed and gave praise to God. They were filled with awe and said, "We have seen remarkable things today."

Luke 5:17–26

Day One: Deep Listening

In this practice, the goal is to simply listen to God through his Word, the Bible. It is a method both of meditating on Scripture and of prayer, of hearing and then responding.

Take a few moments to settle yourself. Take a deep breath, and release any tension in your body. Ask God to meet you and speak to you through this passage.

Read slowly, out loud if possible. Listen for the word or phrase that stands out to you. After you read, spend several minutes in silence. Let the word that stood out echo in your mind and your heart.

Read slowly through the passage again, listening for the word, phrase, or thought that seems to resonate with you. Spend some time simply turning that word or phrase over in your mind. What does God want to say to you? Is there some encouragement or challenge from him in this word? What does he want you to know?

Spend as long as you need in silence, thinking about what God has said. When you are ready, read the passage one more time, listening again for God's word to you. Is there something he wants you to do? Or just to know?

Is he inviting you into a deeper intimacy with himself? Is he asking you to go deeper in your seeking of him and his will? Is he asking you to act on your faith, to make it visible? Reflect on what he's said to you. Let this time lead you into a dialogue with God or a comfortable silence.

End your time by thanking him for speaking with you through his Word. Write a sentence or two on your life card about what God has said to you.

Day Two: Journaling

The paralytic in the story received two healings: first a spiritual healing and then a physical healing. In verse 20, Jesus tells the man his sins are forgiven—which of course gets the Pharisees a bit riled up. By saying that he forgave the man of all his sins, Jesus was claiming to be God. After a discussion with the Pharisees, Jesus also heals the man's physical affliction.

Journal about the following: Where do you need spiritual healing? Are unresolved questions or patterns of behavior keeping you from intimacy with God? Where do you need physical healing? Perhaps you need God to free you from pain, depression, or just exhaustion. Write a note to Jesus asking him for the healing you need.

Day Three: Solitude

One phrase that has become meaningful to me in this passage is "right in front of Jesus" (v. 19). Today, get some time alone—do whatever it takes to leave behind the duties of your work and family and spend some time "right in front of Jesus."

This time of solitude is necessary. It is like oxygen for your soul. Breathe in his presence. Allow the quiet and peace to heal you.

Bring your life card and reflect on what God's been saying to you this week. Feel free to journal on this further if you like, but don't feel obligated. All you want to do is be right in front of Jesus.

The text says that after he was healed, the paralytic "went home praising God" (v. 25). After your solitude time, thank him for the healing power of his presence, and "go home praising God."

Sabbath Reflection

Read the text out loud. Then read slowly through this reflection. It's up to you whether to include your family or others in this practice. If you do include children, depending on their ages, you can read this to them, summarize it, or simply ask them for their observations about the story. If you have a children's Bible, you could read the story from that version. Be open to the idea that they may have some insights that God can use to speak to you. You can use the questions at the end with others or on your own. Use as many or as few of the questions as you like.

The Christian faith was never meant to be a solo journey. Certainly there's an individual aspect to it—we need time alone with God to nurture the personal relationship we have with him. While our faith is personal, it's also relational. Jesus said the key to a life of faith is to love God and love others. Not just God. Sometimes we're tempted to love God and barely tolerate others, but that's not what he wants. Loving others is the key to the abundant life that he's inviting us into.

Life, and life to the full, this fresh air that Jesus is inviting us to breathe in, can't be found in isolation. It's found in community—in loving others, in learning how to get along with them, in helping them. Even others who are imperfect, others who are difficult to love, and others who perhaps can't give back as much as we give to them. People like your children, a stubborn co-worker, a grouchy neighbor, or perhaps your in-laws.

This abundant life of peace and love that Jesus offers—I think it's found in loving others, but also in letting others love you. I think sometimes receiving is harder than giving love—accepting help from others and allowing yourself to need your friends. It takes a certain vulnerability, a letting down of your guard. An admission of neediness, which hardly sounds like the best route to peace and joy and life abundant. But as Jesus said, the life he gives is not like what the world gives. It's a bit different. It's a breath of fresh air.

Jesus gathered people around him, and he told us to do the same. He prayed for oneness within the church. Not loneliness, not individuality, but oneness: people coming together to help each other, to love each other, to give to each other what Jesus would give.

Living the Christian faith (not just believing it in our heads but turning it into loving action) sometimes requires that we carry each other. When our faith is weak or paralyzed, we need our friends to carry us, to put us right in front of Jesus. And when we are willing to do that for others—to carry and encourage and bring them to Jesus—that is when we begin to experience what Jesus was talking about, that life he wanted for us: life abundant.

Luke tells us that the man's friends put him "right in front of Jesus" (v. 19). What would that look like today? Maybe we can't go find Jesus and rip the roof off to get to him. But this passage has more than once inspired me to simply pray for someone. In this type of prayer, I don't go into a lot of detail outlining their aches and pains or try to tell Jesus what he ought to do for them. Jesus knows their pain and knows what they need—often better than I do.

Jesus responded not only to the man on the mat but also to his bold friends, who were so sure that Jesus would heal their friend that they took extreme measures.

And the text says, "when Jesus saw their faith," he responded (v. 20). *Their* faith. Not just the faith of this paralytic but that of his friends. One Bible version says Jesus was "impressed by their bold belief" (v. 20 Message). It's the faith of the friends that inspires Jesus.

The paralytic's friends thought he needed to be healed physically. But Jesus knew the man needed something else first. He needed forgiveness. It's what we all need. So the friends don't tell Jesus, "Make him walk." They simply put the man right in front of Jesus, and they wait. That's the faith I think Jesus is commending. Sure, he was impressed with their persistence and enthusiasm, their boldness. But the fact that they trust Jesus to do whatever is needed—that's what faith really is. They don't dare instruct Jesus but trust that he will know—and do—what is best for their friend.

questions

Do you know someone who is going through a painful or paralyzing situation? How can you put them right in front of Jesus?

Tell about (or journal about) a time when you felt like the people around you carried you to Jesus. How did it affect your faith?

Does your faith feel lonely? Do you find yourself wishing that someone would pray for you and carry you to Jesus? Do you do that for others? How willing are you to let others know about your needs?

Week Sixteen Luke 7:11–17

A Son, and Hope, Resurrected

Soon afterward Jesus went with his disciples to the village of Nain, with a great crowd following him. A funeral procession was coming out as he approached the village gate. The boy who had died was the only son of a widow, and many mourners from the village were with her. When the Lord saw her, his heart overflowed with compassion. "Don't cry!" he said. Then he walked over to the coffin and touched it, and the bearers stopped. "Young man," he said, "get up." Then the dead boy sat up and began to talk to those around him! And Jesus gave him back to his mother.

Great fear swept the crowd, and they praised God, saying, "A mighty prophet has risen among us," and "We have seen the hand of God at work today." The report of what Jesus had done that day spread all over Judea and even out across its borders.

Luke 7:11–17 NLT

Day One: Being There

Read slowly through this short passage and try to picture this scene in your mind. By imagining what happened, you are spending time with Jesus.

Jesus is coming into town, not alone but with a large crowd. As they are coming in, a funeral procession is coming out. Imagine the noise of the two crowds colliding—funerals in those days were not quiet, sniffling affairs but filled with wailing and loud crying, a very outward mourning.

Jesus's crowd may have been loud as well—but in a different way. What would they have sounded like? How were they feeling? How does that suddenly shift when they run into the funeral procession?

As you reflect on the scene, notice Jesus. What is he like? Imagine yourself as the widow. Or imagine yourself as the son, suddenly raised from the dead by Jesus's touch.

Spend time with Jesus by reflecting on this passage. Write one or two truths you notice about Jesus on your life card.

Day Two: Kindness

Women in Jesus's day worked hard, but they had few rights. They often had to look to their husbands, sons, or fathers to take care of them. A widow would depend on her son to care for her financially (and, I imagine, emotionally as well). Losing a child is terrible, but for a widow in Jesus's day, it was devastating.

Do you know any widows? A woman who is alone, who needs to know that someone cares? I'd guess you know a woman who perhaps never married or is divorced. You know a woman who feels like she's going through life alone.

Jesus responds to the pain of this woman with deep sympathy and a miracle. While you may not be able to raise someone from the dead, what can you do to show sympathy and kindness to a woman who is alone? Something as simple as a phone call or a visit may feel like a miracle to a woman who feels lonely.

Today, reach out to a lonely woman. If you think you don't know of one, call a local nursing home and ask if you can visit with someone who doesn't typically get visitors. Even if you yourself are a lonely woman—that will make the connection even more sweet. Take her out for coffee or bring her some flowers. Just sit with her and listen. Treat her as you think Jesus would.

Day Three: Breath Prayer

Jesus brought the widow's son back to life and with him resurrected the woman's hope. Are you facing a situation in your life that seems hopeless? Are you grieving some loss? Perhaps you've lost a parent or grandparent. Maybe you're grieving a child, like the widow—even a child who never was born because of infertility or miscarriage. What do you need from Jesus? He may not give you back that person (at least in this life). But he does want to resurrect your hope.

Let your longings and deepest need become a prayer that you can say in the space of a single breath, and write this prayer on your life card. Carry it with you as a reminder to pray, that Jesus wants to resurrect your hope, and that he is always close to the brokenhearted (Ps. 34:18).

Sabbath Reflection

Read the text out loud. Then read slowly through this reflection. It's up to you whether to include your family or others in this practice. If you do include children, depending on their ages, you can read this to them, summarize it, or simply ask them for their observations about the story. If you have a children's Bible, you could read the

120

story from that version. Be open to the idea that they may have some insights that God can use to speak to you. You can use the questions at the end with others or on your own. Use as many or as few of the questions as you like.

Have you ever felt like hope is dead? Perhaps you haven't lost a child, but maybe some other loss or disappointment has killed or at least deeply wounded your hope. Maybe you feel it's your dreams that have died: Your marriage isn't turning out like you'd hoped, or motherhood isn't as fulfilling as you expected, or you're sad because you don't have either marriage or motherhood, which you desperately want.

In this story, a crowd walking with Jesus encounters a funeral procession. Until they came upon this parade of grief, I think Jesus may have been feeling upbeat. He had just had an encounter with a Roman soldier who asked him to heal a servant just by saying a word. The text says Jesus "was amazed" by the soldier's faith (Luke 7:9). I imagine Jesus thinking, *Yes! They're finally getting it!* and feeling like he hadn't come in vain, that there was such a thing as faith and hope. So he's walking along with his disciples and a large crowd. Jesus is feeling hopeful, the crowd around him is probably chattering about the miracle he just did and the things he's been teaching them. Maybe a few of them are asking him questions, and they're having this great conversation as they walk along.

But then, just outside the city, this happy crowd meets a sorrowful crowd: a funeral procession led by a mother. How does she feel? I can't imagine.

Today the front page of the *Chicago Tribune* showed a picture of a grieving mother—her ten-year-old daughter had been killed by a stray bullet that came through her front window in the city's notorious Englewood neighborhood. She's not the first to be shot accidentally even this month. It is a picture of unspeakable tragedy. Sitting here in my suburban kitchen thirty miles away (but it might as well be another planet), I want to cry. The story

121

is so sad and desperate, I don't even want to read it. I feel so bad for the families affected by the tragedy. But I do so from a distance. That's not what Jesus did.

The text says that when Jesus saw the widow, his heart broke for her. He took on her grief. Her sadness touched him deeply. He didn't just observe it; he felt it. So what does he do? Jesus does not avoid the grieving woman who, according to Hebrew tradition, would have led the funeral procession. He comes right up to her. He feels her pain. "Don't cry," he says (v. 13). And then he does something even stranger.

He reaches out to touch the dead body, which was being carried on an open bier or frame. If there was a coffin, it would have been open, or perhaps the body was just lying on the stretcherlike bier, carried by grieving, wailing pallbearers. Because Jewish laws said anyone who touched a dead body would be unclean for seven days, Jesus's reaching out to touch the body might have drawn a gasp from the crowd. Others in the crowd might have pulled away, giving the funeral procession a wide berth to avoid uncleanness and the discomfort of death and suffering—like I avoid certain neighborhoods in Chicago. But not Jesus.

One commentary notes: "As Jesus came face to face with this widow, he stopped the funeral cortege and stretched out his hand to the figure on the bier. To touch the corpse would render him unclean for a week (Num. 19:11). Jesus, however, is more concerned with alleviating the woman's grief than with his own impurity. The son is no longer dead but restored to life and to the arms of his joyous mother. Before the town's gate, life has met death and overcome it."[1]

This interaction, in a way, is a picture of the incarnation: Jesus came into the world to overcome death. His heart goes out to us. He left perfect holiness to become a person, to die for us. Taking the punishment for our sins would render him unclean in God's eyes, at least for a time. But he is more concerned with alleviating our grief than with his own impurity.

122

The two crowds, the one with Jesus and the funeral procession, are watching this scene. I'm guessing it suddenly got quiet when Jesus spoke to the widow and then walked up to the dead son.

Eugene Peterson translates verse 16 of this passage, "They all realized they were in a place of holy mystery, that God was at work among them. They were quietly worshipful—and then noisily grateful, calling out among themselves, 'God is back, looking to the needs of his people!'" (Message).

When your hope seems dead, Jesus's heart goes out to you. It breaks for you. And he is reaching toward you, comforting you. He wants to heal your heart, to invite you into a place of holy mystery. How will you respond? With quiet worship, then noisy gratitude? Both would be appropriate, because you know that God is looking to your needs, willing to do what it takes to bring hope back to life.

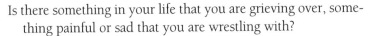

questions

Is there something in your life that you are grieving over, something painful or sad that you are wrestling with?

How can you follow Jesus's example in this story? Do you know someone who is grieving and needs you to reach out to them and embrace them in their pain?

Do you suppose it's possible to wander through "places of holy mystery" and not even be aware of it? What could you do to notice the work of God in your life?

Week Seventeen Luke 7:36–50

Who Loves Much?

When one of the Pharisees invited Jesus to have dinner with him, he went to the Pharisee's house and reclined at the table. A woman in that town who lived a sinful life learned that Jesus was eating at the Pharisee's house, so she came there with an alabaster jar of perfume. As she stood behind him at his feet weeping, she began to wet his feet with her tears. Then she wiped them with her hair, kissed them and poured perfume on them.

When the Pharisee who had invited him saw this, he said to himself, "If this man were a prophet, he would know who is touching him and what kind of woman she is—that she is a sinner."

Jesus answered him, "Simon, I have something to tell you."

"Tell me, teacher," he said.

"Two people owed money to a certain moneylender. One owed him five hundred denarii, and the other fifty. Neither of them had the money to pay him back, so he forgave the debts of both. Now which of them will love him more?"

Simon replied, "I suppose the one who had the bigger debt forgiven."

"You have judged correctly," Jesus said.

Then he turned toward the woman and said to Simon, "Do you see this woman? I came into your house. You did not give me any water for *my feet, but she wet my feet with her tears and wiped them with her hair. You did not give me a kiss, but this woman, from the time I entered, has not stopped kissing my feet. You did not put oil on my head, but she has poured perfume on my feet. Therefore, I tell you, her many sins have been forgiven—as her great love has shown. But whoever has been forgiven little loves little."*

Then Jesus said to her, "Your sins are forgiven."

The other guests began to say among themselves, "Who is this who even forgives sins?"

Jesus said to the woman, "Your faith has saved you; go in peace."

Luke 7:36–50

Day One: Deep Listening

Begin with a simple prayer: "Lord, speak to me through your Word." Spend several minutes just being quiet, letting your mind settle. Put aside concerns, knowing you can deal with them later.

Read the passage through, out loud if possible. Remember that you are not trying to interpret or assign meaning or even figure out how to apply the text. You are simply listening so that God can speak to you.

As you read the passage, listen for which word or phrase leaps off the page, which word stands out most clearly, or the word you are quietly drawn to. Underline it or jot it in the margin.

Read through the passage again, listening again for the word that captures your attention. Ask yourself, "What does God want me to know through this word?"

Read through the passage one more time, again looking and listening for a single word or phrase that stands out. You may hear the same word as you did in the previous reading or perhaps a different word. What is God promising or offering or asking you for through this word?

Take your life card for this week and write the word on it. If you like, add a sentence about how you want to respond to God's word to you. Spend some time thanking him and praising him for meeting you.

Day Two: Breath Prayer

Sit quietly for a few minutes. Be still. You may want to look at your life card, but it's not necessary to do so. If you'd like, read the text again, or just a portion of it.

Think about a name you feel comfortable using for God, Jesus, or the Spirit. It may be inspired by this week's reading or by your own experience. For example, you may want to call God your forgiver, friend, compassionate healer, or kind Father. Then imagine yourself encountering God. Imagine that he asks you, "What do you need? What can I give to you?"

Let your answer come from your deepest desire, your truest self. From the part of you that longs for connection with a God who deeply loves you and wants you to have a full life in the best sense of what that means.

Now combine that name for God with your deep need. A classic breath prayer is, "Lord Jesus, have mercy on me." You may say, "Kind Father, fill me with peace."

Sit quietly, breathe deeply. Turn your sentence into a prayer. It should be brief enough that it can be stated in a single breath.

Repeat it slowly, several times, with restful silence in between.

Write the prayer on your life card. During your week, when you find yourself stressed or hurried, take a moment to pray that one-sentence prayer.

Day Three: Kindness

Jesus said, "Blessed are the poor in spirit" (Matt. 5:3). He says in this week's passage that if you've been forgiven much, you'll love much.

We all need to be forgiven much. It's just we don't always realize it enough. When we do, we'll love much. Simon needed grace just as much as the sinful woman, but his haughty attitude hindered him from receiving forgiveness and love. He chose to ignore his own faults, and thus he chose not to receive the abundance that Jesus could have given him.

Do you ever do that? Is there someone you need to forgive, even if they are not asking for your forgiveness? What attitudes in you might be blocking your ability to receive the love that Jesus wants to give you?

Do one thing: Make a call. Write a note. Forgive someone. Make a meal for someone in your neighborhood—perhaps someone who has recently lost a job or had a baby or is simply overwhelmed. Bring a bag of groceries, some flowers, or a pan of brownies. Be unselfish. If possible, be anonymous. If you have kids, they could draw a card or write a note for the person you are helping. If you're not sure what to do, ask God to show you a need. Then be his hands and feet to meet that need in some small way.

Sabbath Reflection

Read the text out loud. Then read slowly through this reflection. It's up to you whether to include your family or others in this practice. If you do include children, depending on their ages, you can read this to them, summarize it, or simply ask them for their observations about the story. If you have a children's Bible, you could read the story from that version. Be open to the idea that they may have some insights that God can use to speak to you. You can use the questions at the end with others or on your own. Use as many or as few of the questions as you like.

When Jesus lived on earth, wealthy or important people in small towns would sometimes entertain themselves (and their neighbors) by having dinner parties. They'd invite important people and have some interesting conversation.

While not everyone was invited to eat at the party, sometimes people from the town would gather at the home just to listen to the conversation. It was a way for the person hosting the banquet to show off, to honor himself and his guest.

Sometimes poor people would show up, hoping they might not only listen to some interesting conversation but also possibly get some leftover food![1]

The table was usually low to the ground, so people eating at it would either sit on the floor or lie on a low couch or cushions with their head near the table and their feet away from the table. They usually ate with their right hand, leaning on their other elbow. Of course, in those days, they didn't have forks, either.[2]

So Jesus is a guest at one of these parties. He's sitting at the table eating dinner at the house of Simon, a Pharisee. But the woman who comes up to him is not invited. She may have been one of the people there to listen to the conversation, to watch from the sidelines.

The problem was, she didn't stay on the sidelines. Instead, she drew attention to herself and to Jesus. Imagine it: She comes up to Jesus, and since he's probably lying on one of those couches, the first thing she gets to is his feet. She is crying, and her tears get his feet wet. Maybe she doesn't know what to do; she doesn't have a towel. So she uses the only thing she's got: her hair. This was not considered proper behavior—in fact, people would have seen this woman letting her hair down as shocking behavior. She also brings a jar of perfume and pours it on Jesus's feet. Imagine the strong smell of the perfume mingling with the smells of dinner, and the whispers of the people who are watching this. She was making a scene, and the owner of the house didn't like it. Everyone probably felt really uncomfortable. Everyone except Jesus, of course, who just looks at her and lets her continue with this crazy behavior.

The Bible says this woman had lived a sinful life. It wasn't just one or two mistakes. It was a pattern, a lifestyle of promiscuity or, more likely, prostitution. But now she's sorry. Maybe she's already met Jesus before and had a talk with him about how she wants to change her life and start acting the way God wants her to. We don't know. Jesus doesn't seem surprised to see her, so it makes you wonder if they've talked before.

Imagine it: As she comes up to Jesus, maybe people are whispering about her, staring at her. Jesus doesn't push her away, though. Simon, the host of the party, doesn't say anything out loud; he just fumes to himself. But the text says, "Jesus answered him" (v. 40). Did Jesus read Simon's mind or just his expression? Maybe it was fairly obvious what Simon (and everyone else) was thinking.

Jesus knows that Simon, the host, is pretty mad. He knows what people are thinking, even if they try to hide it. So he tells Simon and all the people there at the dinner a story. He wants to teach Simon a lesson, so he tells a parable; it's almost like a riddle. The point of his story is this: If you've really messed up and you get forgiven, you're going to be really grateful. You're going to love the person who forgave you a whole lot.

And if you didn't think you messed up, or if you've been pretty good, then you figure that you don't need as much forgiveness. So you don't feel that grateful.

The point isn't that Simon didn't need forgiveness. In verses 44 to 46, Jesus tells Simon all the ways he has messed up, even just that evening. He didn't show basic kindness or hospitality to Jesus. Simon has sinned, but he's blinded by pride. Because of that, Simon misses out. He doesn't get to experience the love and forgiveness that Jesus wants to give him.

Most of us, I think, wish we could get more love. On our better days we might add that we wish that we were better at giving love. Jesus is saying that to do that, we first have to be willing to admit how we have messed up and ask for his forgiveness.

The last thing Jesus says to the woman is "go in peace" (v. 50). He gives her his peace. She's able to receive it because she has admitted to him her wrongdoing and received his forgiveness. Her sin is gone, and in its place she finds freedom and peace.

questions

Why do you think this woman came to Jesus? What did she think he could give her?

What do you think of Simon? Tell about a time you, like Simon, acted like you were better than someone else.

Tell about a time you did something wrong but then were forgiven. What was that like? Do you agree that when someone forgives you, you love that person more?

Tell about a time you forgave someone. Was it hard to do? What happened to your relationship with that person?

Week Eighteen Luke 10:25–37

Who Is My Neighbor?

One day an expert in religious law stood up to test Jesus by asking him
this question: "Teacher, what must I do to receive eternal life?"

Jesus replied, "What does the law of Moses say? How do you read
it?"

The man answered, "'You must love the Lord your God with all your
heart, all your soul, all your strength, and all your mind.' And, 'Love
your neighbor as yourself.'"

"Right!" Jesus told him. "Do this and you will live!"

The man wanted to justify his actions, so he asked Jesus, "And who
is my neighbor?"

Jesus replied with an illustration: "A Jewish man was traveling on a
trip from Jerusalem to Jericho, and he was attacked by bandits. They
stripped him of his clothes and money, beat him up, and left him half
dead beside the road.

"By chance a Jewish priest came along; but when he saw the man
lying there, he crossed to the other side of the road and passed him by. A
Temple assistant walked over and looked at him lying there, but he also
passed by on the other side.

"Then a despised Samaritan came along, and when he saw the man,
he felt deep pity. Kneeling beside him, the Samaritan soothed his wounds
with medicine and bandaged them. Then he put the man on his own
donkey and took him to an inn, where he took care of him. The next day
he handed the innkeeper two pieces of silver and told him to take care of

the man. 'If his bill runs higher than that,' he said, 'I'll pay the difference the next time I am here.'

"Now which of these three would you say was a neighbor to the man who was attacked by bandits?" Jesus asked.

The man replied, "The one who showed him mercy."

Then Jesus said, "Yes, now go and do the same."

Luke 10:25–37 NLT

Day One: Journaling

Read through the passage slowly. Notice how the priest and the temple assistant (a Levite) responded to the injured man. Now journal for a few minutes about these questions: When have you acted like the priest and the Levite? When have you avoided someone who was going through pain, or when have you just not wanted to get involved in a messy situation? Resist the urge to rationalize your actions. Use this time to confess and to receive God's forgiveness.

Day Two: Being There

Read slowly through the passage. Imagine the rugged desert road Jesus describes. Think about this man who is beaten up and left for dead. The Jews hated the Samaritans. They would not touch them, wouldn't even use the same dishes Samaritans ate out of. Imagine the most racist, bigoted person you know—that's how most Jews acted toward Samaritans. Imagine yourself as the Samaritan, stopping to help someone you knew hated you. Would you be afraid? Would you think, *Why should I help him? He's my enemy. He wouldn't do the same for me.*

Next, take a step back. This story is a parable. Imagine yourself as the expert in the law who listens as Jesus tells this very pointed story. Does it make you uncomfortable?

Write a sentence or two on your life card about this story. For example, you may want to complete this sentence: "If I were the man beaten up, I would feel . . ."

The VeggieTales video *The Story of Flibber-O-Loo* is a delightful retelling of this parable. If you have children, you may want to read the Bible story to them, then watch the video and discuss it with them.

Day Three: Kindness

What does it mean to love your neighbor? After telling the parable, Jesus asks the religious leader if he gets it, if he understands. He does. So Jesus says, "Go and do the same" (v. 37 NLT).

Who is someone you normally would not associate with? Your Samaritan, so to speak. What would it take for you to be kind to someone you might consider an enemy? This week do something kind for someone you normally would not associate with. Reach across social, economic, or racial barriers to extend God's love and grace to someone, even if you know they won't be able to repay you.

After you do this, write the person's name on your life card. Pray for them during the week.

Sabbath Reflection

Read the text out loud. Then read slowly through this reflection. It's up to you whether to include your family or others in this practice.

133

If you do include children, depending on their ages, you can read this to them, summarize it, or simply ask them for their observations about the story. If you have a children's Bible, you could read the story from that version. Be open to the idea that they may have some insights that God can use to speak to you. You can use the questions at the end with others or on your own. Use as many or as few of the questions as you like.

Have you ever felt like someone didn't like you and you really didn't know why? Have you ever been the victim of racism or prejudice? Felt like someone looked down on you because of your economic status or your background?

That's how the Samaritans felt around the Jews. The Jews disdained the Samaritans and thought themselves far superior to people they saw as heathen half-breeds. It was not that different from the way that white people in our country treated African Americans for years. (Only they didn't call them African Americans—the names they used were much less respectful.)

Despite all kinds of talk of "political correctness," racism and prejudice still exist in our country and around the world. Groups of people across the globe hate each other simply because they are of a different race or hold different beliefs. Sometimes the feelings stem from political, religious, or other differences. The feelings of anger and disagreement are real, but that doesn't make the hatred any more logical.

Imagine a black man in America in the 1950s who had perhaps been spit on or had a burning cross put in his front yard. Imagine that man stopping by the side of the road in, say, rural Alabama to help a white man who'd been beaten up—a man he knows is a member of the Ku Klux Klan.

That's the picture Jesus is painting with this parable. The picture of love Jesus paints is not that of a Jew helping a Samaritan (although that would have been a loving thing to do). Loving your neighbor is not about condescending to assist someone you consider lower than yourself on the food chain. The story is even more radical. It's about a *Samaritan* helping a *Jew*—a man of the scorned race helping someone who would have despised him. The one of lower social standing offers care and even money to the one of higher social standing. It's not just loving someone you don't like; it's loving someone who hates you. He did so even though it was likely the man he was helping might not offer to pay him back for his time, trouble, and even money.

The religious man asks Jesus, "What do you mean by *neighbor*?" He's asking a theoretical question. He wants Jesus to give him some rules to recite, some philosophical ideas. I don't think he really wanted to have to put it into action. But Jesus says through this story that definitions and religious rules are not as important as what you do. Loving action is the point. And love must be radical, extravagant, almost illogical. Elsewhere Jesus taught, "Love your enemies and pray for those who persecute you" (Matt. 5:44). That is what this Samaritan was doing—loving his enemy, praying (with his loving action) for one who had likely persecuted him.

Who looks down on you, perhaps for reasons you don't understand? That person, Jesus says, is your neighbor. And I'm asking you to love that person, he notes.

Why does Jesus ask us to love in this way? What on earth would motivate us to do so?

I don't know about you, but I can't love that way just by trying in my own strength to do so. But when I look at Jesus's love for me—even me—that motivates me. His love inspires me. But even then, I still need the Spirit's power to love those who don't love me. This story is a reminder of how Jesus loves us—even when we don't deserve it. You did not earn his love. He gave it even before you knew anything about him. He gave it when you did know about him but chose to go your own way anyhow. Even in the times you may have chosen not to love him (every time you chose your own way over his way), he still loved you.

"You see, at just the right time, when we were still powerless, Christ died for the ungodly. . . . God demonstrates his own love for us in this: While we were still sinners, Christ died for us" (Rom. 5:6, 8).

Jesus calls us to give to others what we have received—unmerited favor—that is, grace. Jesus told his disciples, "Freely have you received, freely give" (Matt. 10:8).

We cannot overcome our own bigotry or prejudice by sheer willpower. We cannot love those who are prejudiced against us by simply wishing to. Jesus offers not only an example but also supernatural power to help us do what we could not do by willpower alone. When we see, really see, what Jesus has done for us, what he has given us—that motivates us to give that same sort of grace to others.

questions

Who is a person whom you find difficult to love? (Perhaps it is someone who has mistreated you, gossiped about you, or criticized you.) What is Jesus asking you to do with this person?

Imagine yourself in the story as the Samaritan and the person you identified in the first question as the injured man. What feelings come to you? Would you do what the Samaritan did for someone who mistreated you?

What point is Jesus trying to make to the man asking "Who is my neighbor"? What do you think he is saying to you personally through this story?

Week Nineteen Luke 13:10–17

A Woman Set Free

On a Sabbath Jesus was teaching in one of the synagogues, and a woman was there who had been crippled by a spirit for eighteen years. She was bent over and could not straighten up at all. When Jesus saw her, he called her forward and said to her, "Woman, you are set free from your infirmity." Then he put his hands on her, and immediately she straightened up and praised God.

Indignant because Jesus had healed on the Sabbath, the synagogue leader said to the people, "There are six days for work. So come and be healed on those days, not on the Sabbath."

The Lord answered him, "You hypocrites! Doesn't each of you on the Sabbath untie your ox or donkey from the stall and lead it out to give it water? Then should not this woman, a daughter of Abraham, whom Satan has kept bound for eighteen long years, be set free on the Sabbath day from what bound her?"

When he said this, all his opponents were humiliated, but the people were delighted with all the wonderful things he was doing.

Luke 13:10–17

Day One: Deep Listening

What does God want to say to you, specifically, through this passage? Begin with a simple prayer: "Lord, speak to me through your Word."

Read the passage through, out loud if possible. Remember that you are not trying to interpret or assign meaning or even figure out how to apply the text. You are not trying to find a universally applicable truth; you're asking God to speak into your personal and unique life. He's able to do that because he knows you intimately. You are simply listening so that God can speak to you.

As you read the passage, listen for which word or phrase leaps off the page, which word stands out most clearly. Underline it or jot it in the margin. Don't try to figure out why that word stands out. Just be patient and listen. Spend a few moments in silence, just quieting your mind and heart. Reflect on the word, but don't try to jump ahead too quickly. Wait.

Read through the passage again, listening again for the word that captures your attention. Ask yourself, What does God want me to know through this word? How does it relate to my life specifically? Again, spend a few moments in silent reflection.

Read through the passage one more time, again looking and listening for a single word or phrase that stands out. You may hear the same word as you did in the previous reading or perhaps a different word. What is God promising or offering or asking you for through this word? Is there an assignment or a promise?

Take your life card for this week and write the word on it. If you like, add a sentence about how you want to respond to God's word to you.

Day Two: Solitude

Make arrangements to spend a chunk of time—an hour or more—alone. Do whatever is necessary to make that happen. Bring your Bible, this book, your life card, perhaps a journal, but nothing else.

Read the passage slowly several times, noticing details. This is the story of a woman who is set free from what had bound her. Take some time to ponder: Where are you bound? Where are you longing for freedom?

Your longing for freedom is—at its deepest level—a longing for God and for truth, the truth that sets us free.

Before her healing, the woman is bent over, unable to stand up straight. What weight are you carrying that has you bent over—literally or figuratively?

In what ways have you allowed yourself to be bound, to be weighed down? What steps could you take to move toward the healing and freedom that Jesus wants to offer you?

Write a sentence or two on your life card about your solitude experience and how God met you in it.

Day Three: Breath Prayer

Jesus's words to the woman in this passage are, "Woman, you are set free from your infirmity" (v. 12). What do you need to be set free from? An addiction? An unhealthy pattern of relating to a friend or family member? Today, pray this breath prayer: "Jesus, set me free." You may want to add a word or two about what specifically you need to be set free from; for example, "Jesus, set me free from worrying about other people's expectations." Or "Jesus, set me free from being critical of others."

Write your breath prayer on your life card and pray it whenever you have a free moment during the week.

Sabbath Reflection

Read the text out loud. Then read slowly through this reflection. It's up to you whether to include your family or others in this practice. If you do include children, depending on their ages, you can read this to them, summarize it, or simply ask them for their observations about the story. If you have a children's Bible, you could read the story from that version. Be open to the idea that they may have some insights that God can use to speak to you. You can use the questions at the end with others or on your own. Use as many or as few of the questions as you like.

Jesus, it appears to me, was a bit of a feminist, in the best sense of that word. He valued and esteemed women, even though he lived in a society that seemed to consider them second-class citizens. While most rabbis would daily pray, "Thank you God that I was not born a Gentile nor a woman," I'm guessing Jesus did not do so. The Bible is full of stories about how he honored women. He often seems to seek out women, hold them up as spiritual examples, and love them in an honorable way.

As a woman and as a person, I want to be valued. I want to know that someone thinks I am important. One of the things I love about Jesus is that he makes it very clear that a person's value is not tied to their race, their religion, their wealth, or their gender. Their value is found in their relationship with God.

This woman had been afflicted with a crippling disease for eighteen years. That's a long time. Still, she runs into Jesus at a local synagogue. Sometimes physical challenges—living in pain—might tempt us to give up on church. To stay away from God and feel sorry for ourselves. But not this woman. She's still showing up, praying for help. For eighteen years. I wonder if I would stay faithful, keep hoping, and keep praying for that long. Or would I grow bitter, cynical, and angry at God?

If I did, I'd be getting angry at the wrong person.

Jesus tells the people that it's not God who has kept this woman tied up in her own body for eighteen years. The battle between good and evil, between God and Satan, is being waged all around us.

Imagine the woman, who perhaps has a severe case of osteoporosis or arthritis. She's bent over, her body twisted in a way that's painful for her and uncomfortable for others to even look at. She's smaller because of her disease. Folded up, almost.

What weighs you down, bends you over, keeps you small? Is it the weight of other people's expectations? Or the burden of trying to make other people happy? Is it the heavy load of living by keeping religious rules, which all seem to imply that "good girls don't make waves"? What is it in your life that has kept you from standing up straight, looking people in the eyes, and believing in your own value? What has stolen your joy?

Maybe your affliction is not physical but emotional or spiritual. Even though others may not be able to see it, it's still painful. It's still keeping you from reaching your full potential.

This woman's society did not value her—in fact, they likely considered her infirmity a punishment for some sin she had committed. Jesus refutes that by his words and his actions.

Catherine Clark Kroeger writes, "Jesus addresses her as 'daughter of Abraham' (Luke 13:16), thereby giving her value as a person of worth and dignity in the kingdom of God. His opponents, however, viewed her as less than human and unworthy of healing on the Sabbath. . . . As a liberated member of the covenant community, she may now stand erect and look people in the face. Those who must hide their faces in shame are they who would deny her this right."[1]

Imagine being that woman, standing up straight for the first time in almost two decades. Picture her expression as she's finally able to straighten and raise her arms—and the first thing she does with them is lift them up in praise to God.

Right now I am realizing that I have lived bent over and small in certain areas of my life. I didn't realize it—I was just trying to avoid conflict, to make certain people happy. In a way, I have been taking the path of least resistance, not wanting to stand up for myself because I was afraid. But doing so has hindered me from standing up and praising God with my life and my actions. It's prevented me from looking people in the eye and feeling the confidence that comes from knowing I am God's beloved daughter.

Jesus sees our struggles and wants to set us free. His words to that woman are his words to you: "You are set free" (v. 12)!

This encounter with Jesus offers hope to anyone who is weary, burdened, and weighed down. He wants to set us free, to lift us up so we can stand up straight, look him in the eyes, and praise him with all of our strength.

questions

Do you ever feel like life has you bent over or weighed down? Explain.

Where are you longing to be set free?

If Jesus were to set you free, what would change in your life? What would it look like? How would it make you feel?

The woman in this story kept showing up at church for eighteen years. She continued to take that small step of faith. What can you do to move toward healing and freedom? What step of faith is God calling you to take? In what way is he asking you to be faithful?

Week Twenty   Luke 15:11–32

Lost and Found

Jesus continued: "There was a man who had two sons. The younger one said to his father, 'Father, give me my share of the estate.' So he divided his property between them.

"Not long after that, the younger son got together all he had, set off for a distant country and there squandered his wealth in wild living. After he had spent everything, there was a severe famine in that whole country, and he began to be in need. So he went and hired himself out to a citizen of that country, who sent him to his fields to feed pigs. He longed to fill his stomach with the pods that the pigs were eating, but no one gave him anything.

"When he came to his senses, he said, 'How many of my father's hired servants have food to spare, and here I am starving to death! I will set out and go back to my father and say to him: Father, I have sinned against heaven and against you. I am no longer worthy to be called your son; make me like one of your hired servants.' So he got up and went to his father.

"But while he was still a long way off, his father saw him and was filled with compassion for him; he ran to his son, threw his arms around him and kissed him.

"The son said to him, 'Father, I have sinned against heaven and against you. I am no longer worthy to be called your son.'

"But the father said to his servants, 'Quick! Bring the best robe and put it on him. Put a ring on his finger and sandals on his feet. Bring the fattened calf and kill it. Let's have a feast and celebrate. For this son of mine was dead and is alive again; he was lost and is found.' So they began to celebrate.

"Meanwhile, the older son was in the field. When he came near the house, he heard music and dancing. So he called one of the servants and asked him what was going on. 'Your brother has come,' he replied, 'and your father has killed the fattened calf because he has him back safe and sound.'

"The older brother became angry and refused to go in. So his father went out and pleaded with him. But he answered his father, 'Look! All these years I've been slaving for you and never disobeyed your orders. Yet you never gave me even a young goat so I could celebrate with my friends. But when this son of yours who has squandered your property with prostitutes comes home, you kill the fattened calf for him!'

"'My son,' the father said, 'you are always with me, and everything I have is yours. But we had to celebrate and be glad, because this brother of yours was dead and is alive again; he was lost and is found.'"

Luke 15:11–32

Day One: Being There

Read through the passage slowly. Then read it again, imagining it in your head like watching a video. Visualize the story from the perspective of the older brother. How does he feel? What does he do with those feelings?

Imagine the story from the father's perspective. Each day his son is gone, he watches for him and perhaps wonders if he should go look for him. How does he feel when his son finally returns?

What about the prodigal son? What motivated him to demand his inheritance early and take off? How does he feel coming home?

Which character do you relate to most in the story? Write one observation about the story on your life card.

Day Two: Kindness

The older brother was unhappy when his father celebrated the younger son's return. Why? Perhaps because he thought his brother did not deserve to be allowed back into the house, let alone have a party thrown in his honor.

It's easy to be kind to someone whom we think "deserves" it. But Jesus tells this story to paint a picture of God's grace: lavish, extravagant, undeserved. Notice the context of this story—it's not a true story but a parable Jesus tells the teachers of the law to answer their criticism that he "welcomes sinners and eats with them" (Luke 15:2).

This week, look for an opportunity to extend kindness to someone who perhaps does not deserve it. Welcome sinners, eat with them, show them extravagant love. Why? Because Jesus did that for you!

Day Three: Solitude

Find some time to get alone by yourself for at least half an hour. The less time you think you can spare this week, the more you need. Read through the passage, and pick one character that you most relate to. What is it that connects you to that character? How are you similar to them? What does Jesus want to say to you through the story? Simply reflect on the story. Let it prompt a conversation with God—not only speaking but also listening. Write a few observations on your life card about what you have heard from God.

Sabbath Reflection

Read the text out loud. Then read slowly through this reflection. It's up to you whether to include your family or others in this practice. If you do include children, depending on their ages, you can read this to them, summarize it, or simply ask them for their observations about the story. If you have a children's Bible, you could read the story from that version. Be open to the idea that they may have some insights that God can use to speak to you. You can use the questions at the end with others or on your own. Use as many or as few of the questions as you like.

In most families, each child will take on a different role. Perhaps you've noticed with your children, nieces and nephews, or friends' children: They are genetically similar, they live in the same environment, and their parents try hard to treat them equitably. Still, they are each very individual. My kids resemble each other physically, but their personalities and temperaments are starkly different. Still, even though they are different, they are much more complex than the labels we may try to put on them: good kid, troublemaker, shy, and so on.

But this is not a story about a real family. It's a parable created in response to an accusation from the religious leaders. "This man welcomes sinners and eats with them," they criticized Jesus in Luke 15:2.

So Jesus tells three stories in Luke 15 to explain why he hangs out with people who seem to be the direct opposite of the religious rule-keepers. He wasn't teaching about how families interact, with different kids taking on different roles. He was saying, "I hang out with sinners because they need grace. And to get real clear about what grace is, here are a few stories about things that were lost getting found."

In the family Jesus creates for his illustration, why does he choose to create the character of the older brother? In his parable the older son is the dutiful, play-by-the-rules, hardworking eldest child. The other is basically a rebellious, wild child.

This younger son demands that his father give him his inheritance early. It's as if he was saying, "Don't make me wait until you die, Pops. Hand over my share of your money now."

We don't hear about the older son's reaction to his brother's antics until later in the story. What did he think? Well, he thought exactly what the Pharisees Jesus was talking to thought: The prodigal is too bad for God to love.

And the prodigal son apparently thought the same thing: "I'm so bad, my Father could never love me." But Jesus uses the story to disprove that thinking.

The older brother also represents faulty thinking about grace. He thinks, "I'm so good, my Father has to love me." That was the way Jesus's audience was thinking; otherwise they would not have objected to his hanging around with sinners.

The parable of the prodigal son is a story to teach us about grace: No sin or rebellion is so great that it can separate us from God's love. I think Jesus has the brother in the story because the converse is also true: Our dutiful rule-keeping won't earn God's love any more than our rebellion will prevent it.

Which brother do you identify with? I, like many eldest children, saw myself as the dutiful overachiever, at least for a while.

But in my early twenties, I questioned everything. I played that prodigal role, or at least it felt like that to me. I didn't reject God, necessarily. I wanted his favor but not his rules. I still talked to him but didn't really listen very much. My prayer life during that season was not conversational. It was more like I was sending postcards. I was self-centered rather than God-centered.

Eventually God sought me out and wooed me back. But I didn't want to return to the older brother mode. Instead, what I longed for and found was the grace of a relationship with God. I was done thinking I could be good enough that God would have to love me.

148

I think most of us can relate in some way to both brothers in the story: We all get confused about grace, thinking we can blow it with our mistakes or earn it with our rule-keeping. But grace is God's unmerited favor. It's getting what we don't deserve: his unconditional love. We can't earn it.

When we choose the wrong path, whether it's for a day or a season, we break God's heart. This story shows us the Father's heart toward us, his wayward children. He stands scanning the horizon, longing to be with us.

This has always been true. Even when the nation of Israel, his chosen people, rebelled against him, God responded with grace. "I will give them a heart to know me, that I am the LORD. They will be my people, and I will be their God, for they will return to me with all their heart" (Jer. 24:7).

God's heart is broken when we wander, and he longs for us to return. A heart can't be broken unless it loves. But God is not indifferent to us. He desires intimacy with us. God is heartbroken by our rebellion because he loves us so much.

He loves to see us make good choices, of course. But he wants those choices to be motivated by love. And that's the most important choice we can make: to extend the grace we've been given to others.

God's heart toward us shapes our identity, regardless of the roles we play or mistakes we make: "How great is the love the Father has lavished on us, that we should be called children of God! And that is what we are!" (1 John 3:1 NIV).

questions

Have you ever felt like no one seems to appreciate how amazingly good you are (the "I'm so good, God has to love me" philosophy)?

Have you ever felt like the prodigal? Have you ever run away from God, thinking life without his rules (guidance) would be more fun? What was that like? Are you in that season now?

Have you ever felt like the prodigal when he longed to go home (felt like "I'm so bad, God could never love me")?

How does it feel to know that God longs for intimacy with you? What step do you want to take today to move closer to him?

Week Twenty-one Luke 22:54–62

Failing at Friendship

Then seizing him, they led him away and took him into the house of the high priest. Peter followed at a distance. And when some there had kindled a fire in the middle of the courtyard and had sat down together, Peter sat down with them. A servant girl saw him seated there in the firelight. She looked closely at him and said, "This man was with him."

But he denied it. "Woman, I don't know him," he said.

A little later someone else saw him and said, "You also are one of them."

"Man, I am not!" Peter replied.

About an hour later another asserted, "Certainly this fellow was with him, for he is a Galilean."

Peter replied, "Man, I don't know what you're talking about!" Just as he was speaking, the rooster crowed. The Lord turned and looked straight at Peter. Then Peter remembered the word the Lord had spoken to him: "Before the rooster crows today, you will disown me three times." And he went outside and wept bitterly.

Luke 22:54–62

Day One: Journaling

Read through the passage. Then look back at Luke 22:31–34. Peter had made a promise that he would follow Jesus anywhere, even to death. He didn't keep his promise of faithfulness to Jesus. Write down a handful of promises you've made to God in your life. Have you kept those promises? When you broke a promise to be faithful to God, how did that feel? What happened to your relationship with God? Write for five minutes without stopping or editing yourself—describe what happened and how you felt about it.

Day Two: Deep Listening

Begin by praying this simple prayer: "Lord, speak to me through your Word."

Read through the passage slowly. If you have more time, you may want to read more of the chapter to provide context, but then focus on verses 54–62. What does God want to say to you specifically through this passage? You're not trying to learn about Peter or mankind in general but rather trying to listen to what God is saying to you personally.

Read the passage through again, out loud if possible. Remember that you are not trying to interpret or assign meaning or even figure out how to apply the text. You are asking God to speak into your personal and unique life. He's able to do that because he knows you intimately. You are simply listening so that God can speak to you.

As you read the passage, listen for which word or phrase leaps off the page, which word stands out most clearly. Underline it or jot it in the margin. Don't try to figure out why that word stands out. Just be patient and listen.

Ask yourself, What does God want me to know through this word? How does it relate to my life specifically? Again, spend a few moments in silent reflection.

Read through the passage one more time, again looking and listening for a single word or phrase that stands out. You may hear the same word as you did in the previous reading or perhaps a different word. What is God promising or offering or asking you to do? Is there an assignment or a promise?

Take your life card for this week and write the word on it. If you like, add a sentence about how you want to respond to God's word.

Day Three: Breath Prayer

God is always faithful to us, but we are not always faithful to him. We may not outright deny him, but in certain situations we may not speak up to defend him or admit that we know him. We may not be willing to admit that we are a friend of Jesus because we're worried others will think we are strange or fanatical.

Write on your life card a breath prayer that expresses your desire to be faithful to Jesus and your appreciation for his faithfulness to you. When you are tempted to deny him or just avoid talking about him, pull out your card, take a few deep breaths, and pray. Then listen for his direction and act on it.

Sabbath Reflection

Read the text out loud. Then read slowly through this reflection. It's up to you whether to include your family or others in this practice.

153

If you do include children, depending on their ages, you can read this to them, summarize it, or simply ask them for their observations about the story. If you have a children's Bible, you could read the story from that version. Be open to the idea that they may have some insights that God can use to speak to you. You can use the questions at the end with others or on your own. Use as many or as few of the questions as you like.

Peter is criticized for the way he behaves, but I have a question: Where are the other disciples at this point?

The Gospel of John says that another disciple went with Peter, most likely John himself (see John 18:15). But it seems that the others have scattered. Peter, in spite of his failings, at least followed Jesus as he was taken away. At first he stays in the shadows, but when a few servants light a fire for warmth, he walks into the courtyard (or front yard) of the high priest's house, where Jesus is being questioned. He's even so bold as to sit down by the fire. What's going through his mind? What did he think would happen? Did he expect anyone to ask who he was or what he was doing there? What did he plan to say?

Or maybe he just acted without thinking. Other stories of Peter in the Bible tell us he was a bit impulsive. Maybe he didn't have a plan, he just followed his gut. Maybe he wanted to be faithful. He wanted to show Jesus that he was a good friend. Earlier Jesus had told him to take a sword (see Luke 22:36); maybe Peter was waiting for Jesus to suddenly confront his accusers, to resist them. Maybe Peter wanted to be there to fight for Jesus—to defend him, help him, do something. He was a man of action.

After all, those in the courtyard were apparently able to look into the house to see what was going on. And those inside could see the people out front. After Peter had denied Jesus, verse 61 says, "The Lord turned and looked straight at Peter." Oh, man. Can you imagine? The thing you swore you wouldn't do, you just did. The man you said you'd die for, you just betrayed. And he's right there, being questioned and insulted by the religious leaders. And he turns, sad eyes locking with yours. What did those eyes say to Peter? *You just broke my heart, Peter, because I love you.*

The next verse says, "Then Peter remembered" (v. 61).

When my kids make a mistake or misbehave, they will usually feel remorse, or at least regret it when they get caught. When we talk about it, they'll admit that they made a bad choice. They will sometimes claim that they "forgot" the rules, that they didn't remember what they were supposed to do. "You know we don't hit our friends, right?" I ask. "I forgot!" they cry.

Peter, hit by that look from Jesus, suddenly remembers. Not only does he remember what Jesus predicted about the denial, but I think he remembers a lot more. He remembers all of it, like his life flashing before his eyes: being told he would fish for souls, not fish; the miracles he witnessed; the teaching and conversations; seeing Jesus transfigured on a mountain; walking on water, for heaven's sake. It all comes back—three years of adventure with Jesus, his life supposedly forever changed. He remembers. And then he goes outside and weeps bitterly.

Sometimes I forget. And I don't make the right choices. I may not deny Jesus out loud, but my actions and attitudes do. I get proud or haughty. I put much more effort into image management than into soul connections. I focus on the wrong things. I forget about focusing on Jesus. I forget.

What will help me to remember? As hard as it is, I need to have the courage to do what Peter did: to look at Jesus. To let him see me and to see him. I need to look into the eyes of the one who loves me. Loves me even when I'm making bad choices. Loves me even when I get scared and don't stand up for him or for what's right. Loves me when I'm angry and impatient with my kids, who have "forgotten" how to behave again.

When we look at Jesus, we remember his love for us.

questions

What feelings or reactions does this story stir in you? Can you relate to Peter? Why or why not?

In what ways do you "deny" the people you love?

Have you ever felt scared to stand up for someone or something? What happened?

Week Twenty-two   John 4:1–26

Bridging the Divide

Jesus realized that the Pharisees were keeping count of the baptisms that he and John performed (although his disciples, not Jesus, did the actual baptizing). They had posted the score that Jesus was ahead, turning him and John into rivals in the eyes of the people. So Jesus left the Judean countryside and went back to Galilee.

To get there, he had to pass through Samaria. He came into Sychar, a Samaritan village that bordered the field Jacob had given his son Joseph. Jacob's well was still there. Jesus, worn out by the trip, sat down at the well. It was noon.

A woman, a Samaritan, came to draw water. Jesus said, "Would you give me a drink of water?" (His disciples had gone to the village to buy food for lunch.)

The Samaritan woman, taken aback, asked, "How come you, a Jew, are asking me, a Samaritan woman, for a drink?" (Jews in those days wouldn't be caught dead talking to Samaritans.)

Jesus answered, "If you knew the generosity of God and who I am, you would be asking me for a drink, and I would give you fresh, living water."

The woman said, "Sir, you don't even have a bucket to draw with, and this well is deep. So how are you going to get this 'living water'? Are you a better man than our ancestor Jacob, who dug this well and drank from it, he and his sons and livestock, and passed it down to us?"

Jesus said, "Everyone who drinks this water will get thirsty again and again. Anyone who drinks the water I give will never thirst—not ever.

The water I give will be an artesian spring within, gushing fountains of endless life."

The woman said, "Sir, give me this water so I won't ever get thirsty, won't ever have to come back to this well again!"

He said, "Go call your husband and then come back."

"I have no husband," she said.

"That's nicely put: 'I have no husband.' You've had five husbands, and the man you're living with now isn't even your husband. You spoke the truth there, sure enough."

"Oh, so you're a prophet! Well, tell me this: Our ancestors worshiped God at this mountain, but you Jews insist that Jerusalem is the only place for worship, right?"

"Believe me, woman, the time is coming when you Samaritans will worship the Father neither here at this mountain nor there in Jerusalem. You worship guessing in the dark; we Jews worship in the clear light of day. God's way of salvation is made available through the Jews. But the time is coming—it has, in fact, come—when what you're called will not matter and where you go to worship will not matter.

"It's who you are and the way you live that count before God. Your worship must engage your spirit in the pursuit of truth. That's the kind of people the Father is out looking for: those who are simply and honestly themselves before him in their worship. God is sheer being itself—Spirit. Those who worship him must do it out of their very being, their spirits, their true selves, in adoration."

The woman said, "I don't know about that. I do know that the Messiah is coming. When he arrives, we'll get the whole story."

"I am he," said Jesus. "You don't have to wait any longer or look any further."

John 4:1–26 Message

Day One: Being There

In this practice, remember, you are simply engaging your imagination. Your goal is not to interpret the text or determine its meaning. Rather, your objective is to make the text come alive by simply entering the story.

Read the text slowly, out loud if possible. Imagine yourself as the woman at the well. What are you thinking about? How are you feeling? It's the middle of the day in a desert region—imagine the heat, the smells. Maybe someone has brought their camels there to get water and their scent lingers in the dusty air. Imagine the rope in your hands as you lower a bucket into the well and the weight and roughness of it as you pull it up full of water. As that woman, what do you notice about Jesus? As the conversation progresses, how do you feel? Does Jesus make you feel comfortable or nervous?

Read the story again, this time as if you were an unseen observer. What do you notice about Jesus and the woman? What stirs in your soul as you watch Jesus speak to this woman? How does he treat her? How does she treat him? What is she like? What is Jesus like?

Do not jump to interpret or draw conclusions. After meditating on the story for a while, simply thank Jesus for the opportunity to spend time with him. If you like, write a sentence on your life card that describes Jesus based on your interaction with him. You may want to write, "Jesus is kind," or "Jesus is puzzling sometimes."

Day Two: Breath Prayer

Read just verses 10–14, slowly, two or three times. Does your life feel dry? Are you thirsty for living water?

Jesus says that he gives us living water. He is what our souls are thirsty for. Are you thirsty? Spend a little time just thinking about your spiritual thirst. What are you thirsty for?

Take some time to just be still, to breathe slowly and deeply. As you exhale, let go of any worries or concerns. As you inhale, think of being filled by the Spirit, drinking in God's presence. Use the phrase "living water" as a way of focusing on Jesus. If you like, you may imagine a spring, pool, waterfall, or some other image of water. Imagine drinking deeply of sweet, cold water. You may want to put this phrase into a request to Jesus, praying, "Jesus, give me living water." Or simply let the phrase itself, "living water," be your only thought.

Let go of any distractions. Simply think about Jesus. If your mind wanders, use the phrase "living water" to bring your thoughts back to your prayer—an expression of your desire to be in his presence.

End your time of reflection by thanking Jesus for being with you. If you like, write an observation or two about this on your life card. When life gets busy, pull out the card and remember the peacefulness of this moment.

Day Three: Kindness

Writer Donald Miller reflects on this passage: "John includes in his gospel an interaction between Jesus and a woman from Samaria. She was from a group of people known in the day for subscribing to loose interpretation of the Judaic system; the modern day evangelical equivalent of a Unitarian. In the scene, Jesus is alone with this woman at a well, where He has come for a drink and she has come to draw water for the day. The woman has a loose reputation, according to the text, having gone through five husbands. In this day, it was nearly unheard of for Jews to have any dealings at all with Samaritans, much less women of her repute. . . . A friend recently told me that this exchange would be the equivalent of a known evangelical walking into a gay bar and asking a man to buy him a beer."[1]

Jesus lived in a very segregated society, yet he reached across society's barriers to talk to a woman of a different race, a different class. He was a Jewish holy man; she was a Samaritan floozy. Do you have relationships with people who are different from you—in a different social class or of a different race? Do you know anyone who, like this Samaritan woman, seems unable to commit to one man? Who doesn't believe the same things you do or act in a way you think is proper? Who has different political views than you do? How do you think Jesus would treat that person? How can you offer kindness, a cup of cold water, to those who are different from you? Today, find a way to interact with someone you normally would not even talk to. Notice what happens to your soul when you do so. How does this affect the fullness of your life? Make a note on your life card about what happens.

Sabbath Reflection

Read the text out loud. Then read slowly through this reflection. It's up to you whether to include your family or others in this practice. If you do include children, depending on their ages, you can read this to them, summarize it, or simply ask them for their observations about the story. If you have a children's Bible, you could read the story from that version. Be open to the idea that they may have some insights that God can use to speak to you. You can use the questions at the end with others or on your own. Use as many or as few of the questions as you like.

In this week's story, Jesus has a public conversation with a woman. The text tells us his disciples were surprised when they returned to see him talking to a woman. Men, especially those who were religious leaders, like Jesus, simply didn't talk to women in public. Jesus was Jewish, and Jews would not talk to Samaritans or even use the same dishes that Samaritans would use. It was like they were afraid of getting Samaritan germs. Jews disdained Samaritans—didn't want to even touch things they had touched.

That's why the woman is surprised that Jesus even speaks to her, let alone asks her for a drink. In order to get a drink from the Samaritan woman, he'd not only have to ask her, he'd have to drink from her water jug.

You may think, well, Jesus was God, so it was easier for him to be kind and to reach out to people from other cultures. Yes, Jesus was a very loving person. He was God. But he was also a human being.

Why does Jesus sit by the well? The Bible says it is because he was tired. Yes, he was God, but while he was here on earth, he felt and lived like a person. He got tired, and he was thirsty. You'd think someone who was God would never get weary. But he did.

Jesus's tiredness gives us a glimpse of his humanity. He wrestled with the things we wrestle with. At times he got tired, frustrated, or angry. So Jesus has to decide whether he will be kind or not, whether he will reach out to someone who is very different from him or not.

Sometimes when I am tired, I don't feel like being nice. I don't feel like making an effort to get to know someone or trying to be friendly with someone from another culture, someone who is different from me. It can be a little intimidating and feels like it would take more energy than I have at that moment.

But if we want to live God's way, we'll look at the things Jesus did and try to act as he would. Jesus could have ignored the woman. That's what other people, including his disciples, would have expected. It's what the woman expected, which is why she's surprised to find herself having a conversation with Jesus.

Jesus showed us how to live. Stories like this one teach us what Jesus was like, but more importantly, how we ought to act. It's part of what it means to love Jesus and follow him—we do what he would. And Jesus loved people, even people who were different from him. It's why people thought he was so amazing: He didn't always tell people what they wanted to hear, but he always paid attention to people, even those whom others ignored.

You can ignore people who are different from you. But Jesus asks us to love others. Not just people who are exactly like us but *all* others: friends and those who are not our friends. In case we didn't understand that idea, he showed us how to do it.

questions

Whom do you choose as friends? Are they people like you or different from you? Do you think this woman was a lot like Jesus or very different from him?

What do you think this woman was really "thirsty" for?

What are you thirsty for? What is it that you long for most in life?

If you are doing this reflection with kids, you can ask them something like this: Are there kids at school or people in your neighborhood you normally wouldn't bother talking to? You may not be mean to them (hopefully!), but you aren't kind either. Maybe you laugh at them or whisper when they walk by. Or maybe you just ignore them. How do you think Jesus would treat those people?

Week Twenty-three John 4:43–54

Take Him at His Word

After the two days he left for Galilee. (Now Jesus himself had pointed out that prophets have no honor in their own country.) When he arrived in Galilee, the Galileans welcomed him. They had seen all that he had done in Jerusalem at the Passover Festival, for they also had been there.

Once more he visited Cana in Galilee, where he had turned the water into wine. And there was a certain royal official whose son lay sick at Capernaum. When this man heard that Jesus had arrived in Galilee from Judea, he went to him and begged him to come and heal his son, who was close to death.

"Unless you people see signs and wonders," Jesus told him, "you will never believe."

The royal official said, "Sir, come down before my child dies."

"Go," Jesus replied, "your son will live."

The man took Jesus at his word and departed. While he was still on the way, his servants met him with the news that his boy was living. When he inquired as to the time when his son got better, they said to him, "Yesterday, at one in the afternoon, the fever left him."

Then the father realized that this was the exact time at which Jesus had said to him, "Your son will live." So he and his whole household believed.

This was the second sign Jesus performed after coming from Judea to Galilee.

John 4:43–54

Day One: Solitude

Do whatever you need to do in order to get some time alone. Start planning for it a day or two in advance. If possible, get out of the house. Let someone else care for children or other obligations, even if it's only for an hour or so. If you work outside the home, you may feel guilty for taking part of a day off to be away from your responsibilities at work and at home. But give yourself this gift—oxygen for your soul that will strengthen you to love others better.

Begin your time alone with a simple prayer of thanks that you are indeed getting to spend some time alone with Jesus. Ask him to meet with you and to meet your deepest needs through this time.

Read through the passage slowly. Spend some time pondering the truth of the story. Is there a situation you're facing that feels as if it needs a miracle? Are Jesus's words to the official true of you—that is, does your faith depend on "signs and wonders"? Or can you have hope in things unseen?

Write a sentence or two on your life card, recording any insights or questions that arise.

Day Two: Being There

Read slowly through the passage. Remember that in this practice, you are using your imagination to enter the story as a way of spending time with Jesus. Create a short video in your mind, watching the scene unfold. Put yourself into various roles in the scene. Take five or ten minutes to imagine the scene, to "daydream" about it. This is simply a way of meditating on Scripture. Add details—what smells and sounds surround the action described? Use your five senses as you put yourself into the story: What do you see, hear, feel, taste, smell?

What do you notice about Jesus? What is he like? What does his response to the man's request tell you about him? What do you think he is feeling and thinking? What attracts you to him or rubs you the wrong way? What do you want to thank Jesus for in your own life?

Write an observation, based on this meditation, on your life card.

Day Three: Breath Prayer

Jesus, as we see in this passage and elsewhere, is a life-giver and a healer. What else do you notice about Jesus in this passage? Choose one word or phrase, such as "life-giver," and reflect on it. What situation are you facing that you need Jesus to breathe life into? Let your desire well up into a single-sentence prayer. Take a few minutes to simply breathe deeply and slowly, to quiet your soul. When you are ready, say your prayer on a single breath. Be silent for a while, focusing on Jesus. If you get distracted or worried, say the breath prayer again as a means of focusing and to express the deepest desire of your soul.

Write your prayer on your life card. Pray it throughout the week.

Sabbath Reflection

Read the text out loud. Then read slowly through this reflection. It's up to you whether to include your family or others in this practice. If you do include children, depending on their ages, you can read this to them, summarize it, or simply ask them for their observations about the story. If you have a children's Bible, you could read the story from that version. Be open to the idea that they may have some insights that God can use to speak to you. You can use the questions at the end with others or on your own. Use as many or as few of the questions as you like.

This interaction with a royal official happens a few days after Jesus's conversation with the woman at the well. The official and the woman were as different as two people could be. Yet both have an interaction with Jesus that leads them to faith and then leads others to faith as well.

The Samaritan woman (see last week's study) was at the bottom of the social ladder. She was despised for her ethnicity, not even considered a person because of her gender, and whispered about unkindly because of her loose lifestyle. She was likely poor. She asked Jesus for nothing and was shocked when Jesus asked *her* for a drink of water. But after a gently confrontational conversation, she puts her faith in him. And not only that, but because of her testimony, Jesus stayed two days in Samaria, preaching with great results. The text says many "believed in him because of the woman's testimony" (John 4:39). Converted one day, she became an evangelist the next.

The official, on the other hand, was a wealthy, influential man with power and political pull. He would have been perhaps used to being in authority, often telling people what to do and having them do it.

He doesn't seem to approach Jesus that way. It says he "begged" Jesus to come and heal his son (v. 47).

Jesus's response is curious: He somehow sees that the man is simply looking for some sort of magic. This man, being a royal official, was likely a Gentile. He may have had no connection to the spiritual in his mind at that point—only a wish for some sort of incantation that would restore his son's health. He sees Jesus as a miracle worker but not as the Messiah. He was looking for a fix, not for faith.

Imagine what this man was thinking. He'd left his very ill son at home in Capernaum and walked twenty miles over the hilly terrain of Galilee to Cana, apparently because he'd heard a miracle worker was there.[1] As a royal official, he had servants (see v. 51). He could have sent a servant to fetch Jesus. But as a father, he wants to go to Jesus himself. Perhaps he has a sense of Jesus's power. What is he feeling as he makes his request? What does Jesus's initial rebuff do to his hopes? Is he crushed, or is he just annoyed that this rabbi won't listen to him?

Sometimes I wonder if part of the conversation in both of these interactions got left out of the Bible. Or perhaps it was so private that it wasn't recorded because only Jesus and the individual knew about it. What else did Jesus say to the official? To the woman? Or was there a knowing, a connection when each of them looked into the face of Jesus, and suddenly everything changed? I think maybe it was both. The woman's search for love and affirmation ended when she found pure love; the official's shallow understanding somehow deepened into faith. Both somehow realized that Jesus was more than they thought, and knowing that demanded a response.

The official, rather than be offended by Jesus's rebuke, continues to beg him to heal his son. Jesus seems to sense some change in the man—that's what makes me think there may have been more to their conversation. And he tells him to go home, his son will be healed.

The text says, "The man took Jesus at his word and departed" (v. 50). He took him at his word. He believed that his son would be healed. He didn't just believe this in theory; it says the man departed. He headed home. He put his newfound faith into action. What happened to cause such a change?

At home he learns that his son's fever broke at the exact time that Jesus had promised it would. As a result, the text says, "he and his whole household believed" (v. 53). A royal official's household was not just his wife and two kids. It was likely a large household of immediate and extended family and servants. Here's another place where we don't have a record of the conversation between the official and his family. Just knowing that the son was healed at the moment Jesus said so would perhaps have led them to the type of "faith" the official had going in—that Jesus was a miracle worker. It would have been interesting, but I don't think that alone would have been enough to make all those people believe in Jesus.

I don't know, but I'll bet that official came away from his interaction with Jesus changed. Jesus rebuked him but then loved him anyway. Perhaps Jesus helped him understand the difference between thinking someone is able to do a miracle and putting all your trust in a relationship with that person.

Everyone in the official's household *believed*. Many in the woman's Samarian town *believed*. Believed what? The New Living Translation says that in both cases, they "believed in Jesus" (vv. 39 and 53). They believed that he was "the Savior of the world" (v. 42) and that faith in him would save them. Both the woman and the official had an interaction with Jesus that was like a breath of fresh air, leaving them (and others they shared the truth with) forever changed.

questions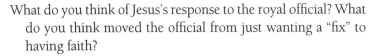

What do you think of Jesus's response to the royal official? What do you think moved the official from just wanting a "fix" to having faith?

Have you ever taken Jesus at his word? Describe that situation. What convinced you to believe that Jesus would come through for you?

What do you think the official told his family and servants when he got home to explain how his son had been healed?

Week Twenty-four John 5:1–15

"Do You Want to Get Well?"

Some time later, Jesus went up to Jerusalem for one of the Jewish festivals. Now there is in Jerusalem near the Sheep Gate a pool, which in Aramaic is called Bethesda and which is surrounded by five covered colonnades. Here a great number of disabled people used to lie—the blind, the lame, the paralyzed. One who was there had been an invalid for thirty-eight years. When Jesus saw him lying there and learned that he had been in this condition for a long time, he asked him, "Do you want to get well?"

"Sir," the invalid replied, "I have no one to help me into the pool when the water is stirred. While I am trying to get in, someone else goes down ahead of me."

Then Jesus said to him, "Get up! Pick up your mat and walk." At once the man was cured; he picked up his mat and walked.

The day on which this took place was a Sabbath, and so the Jewish leaders said to the man who had been healed, "It is the Sabbath; the law forbids you to carry your mat."

But he replied, "The man who made me well said to me, 'Pick up your mat and walk.'"

So they asked him, "Who is this fellow who told you to pick it up and walk?"

The man who was healed had no idea who it was, for Jesus had slipped away into the crowd that was there.

Later Jesus found him at the temple and said to him, "See, you are well again. Stop sinning or something worse may happen to you." The man went away and told the Jewish leaders that it was Jesus who had made him well.

John 5:1–15

Day One: Deep Listening

Begin by sitting for a moment or two in silence. Take your time. Take a few deep breaths, breathing slowly: in through the nose, out through the mouth. Slow your breathing, and let your mind take its cue from your body. Let go of the to-do list that might be trying to race through your head.

Ask God to speak to you through his Word. Trust that he will.

Read through the text slowly, out loud if possible. Let the words wash over you. Listen for the word or phrase that jumps off the page at you. Underline it if you like.

Read the text a second time, listening for a word or phrase that stands out. Pray as you read. Ask God to meet you in the text, to show you what he wants you to know or to be. Write the phrase in your journal or in the margins of this book, and spend a few moments pondering it, repeating the words, listening for what God wants to tell you in those words.

When you are ready, read the text one more time. You may want to narrow your focus in on one or two paragraphs. Is God inviting you to take a step of faith through this passage? What is he asking you to do? Pray that God would give you the strength to take the step he is asking you to take.

Thank God for meeting you in his Word. If you like, write a word or sentence on your life card to remind you of this interaction with Jesus.

Day Two: Journaling

The man in this story is a complicated character. Jesus asks him an interesting question, "Do you want to get well?" (v. 6), which the man does not answer, except with excuses.

Pick any or all of the following questions and simply write your response in your journal. Don't edit yourself—there are no right or wrong answers here. Keep writing for at least two minutes, longer if you like.

How do you respond to this man? What do you think of him? Why has he been lying by that pool for thirty-eight years?

In what ways are you like that man? If you were in his situation, how would you have responded to Jesus's question? How do you respond to it in your own life? What do you need to be healed of? In what area—perhaps emotional, spiritual, or physical—do you need to "get well"?

Day Three: Breath Prayer

This passage shows that Jesus is a healer not just of bodies but of our souls. And sometimes healing comes from Jesus's loving confrontation—it may be that our attitude, like this man's, is what needs the most help. Spend some time simply thinking about Jesus and his healing touch. Invite Jesus the healer to be with you.

What name for Jesus comes to mind as you reflect on this aspect of his character? Look at your journal entry from day two of this week. What desire simmers underneath your thoughts, longings, musings? What do you notice is true of you? What do you need? Now combine your name for Jesus with that desire into a sentence or breath prayer. For example, you might pray, "Great Physician, help me to reconcile my relationship with . . ." or "Compassionate Healer, release my body from pain," or "Jesus, I need your help to heal me of my anger."

Write your prayer on your life card, and when you feel that need or desire bubbling up, take a few deep breaths and pray it, out loud if you like.

Sabbath Reflection

Read the text out loud. Then read slowly through this reflection. It's up to you whether to include your family or others in this practice. If you do include children, depending on their ages, you can read this to them, summarize it, or simply ask them for their observations about the story. If you have a children's Bible, you could read the story from that version. Be open to the idea that they may have some insights that God can use to speak to you. You can use the questions at the end with others or on your own. Use as many or as few of the questions as you like.

When I read this passage, the phrase that jumps out at me and the question that continues to reverberate in my mind as I go through my days is, "Do you want to get well?" (v. 6).

It seems an odd question at first. This man is lying by a pool called Bethesda, which was alleged to have healing powers. Some texts say that an angel would occasionally stir the water, and the first one to scramble to the water would be healed. Imagine it—it almost seems like a Monty Python movie scene as blind, paralyzed, and otherwise afflicted people trip over each other in an effort to dive into a pool they believe will heal them. It's almost comic, in a pathetic kind of way.

So this guy's been by the pool for thirty-eight years. Thirty-eight! Little wonder, then, that Jesus asks, "Um, do you really want to get well? If so, why are you still here?" Of course, that also seems a little cruel. After all, we have to assume the man has tried. In fact, he's full of excuses: "No one is helping me; everyone else always gets there first."

But you have to wonder, did this guy ask for help? One of the keys to recovery is learning to ask for help. This pool wasn't in some remote area on the outskirts of town; it was in the middle of Jerusalem, with lots of people around. Did he ask for help?

I have to think this guy had some issues. Instead of answering Jesus directly, he makes excuses. He doesn't say, "Oh yes, I do want to get well." He starts moaning and complaining.

So for almost forty years, he's been lying by this pool, watching other people get healed while he is not. And apparently everyone knew him—Jesus "learned" the man's story (v. 6). Maybe he learned it from other people who told him, "Oh, that's the old-timer, the guy who's been here thirty-eight years." Maybe the man took a certain pride in being the elder statesman of the cripples by the pool. I don't know.

The text says people with all sorts of disabilities hung out there—blind, paralyzed, lame. This man, John says, was an "invalid" (v. 5). So we don't know what afflicted him. You'd think John would have called him a blind man or a paralytic if that's what he was. But he doesn't, so we can't say. But what if he was one of those people who is just always complaining about their aches and pains and relishes the role of the victim and the attention that comes with that just a bit?

If so, what if Jesus was a little frustrated with this guy. "Get up!" he says (v. 8). Quit moaning. When the Jews question the man, again he refuses to take responsibility for himself. "That man who made me well," he begins (v. 11), as if to say, "He *made* me get well; it's his fault. He *told* me to pick up my mat."

174

Jesus runs into him later and warns him, "Stop sinning" (v. 14). In other words, Jesus says, "I've done what I can for you. Now it is up to you to change your attitude."

I can feel pretty smug about this guy's issues—until I realize Jesus's word to me is, "Do you want to get well?" Patterns of sin, which are my responsibility, have been hanging around in my life—some of them for a long time. It's tempting to complain: "No one is helping me." To blame my struggles on other people, who *make* me behave the way I do. But do I really want to be healthy? Do I want to give up my sinful patterns, my addiction to other people's approval, my attempts to control? Complaining about the people who are not helping me has become a sort of comforting habit. Do I really, really want to be well? If I do, I have to listen to Jesus, who says, "Get up! It's a new day, and you need to carry your own burdens and walk on your own two feet."

It's not an easy thing for me to hear, but it's ultimately the kindest thing he could say.

questions

How would you describe the attitude of the man before he gets healed? Does his attitude change after he's healed?

If Jesus were to say to you, "Do you want to get well?" what specifically do you think he would be referring to?

Week Twenty-five John 7:1–13

Unbelieving Brothers

After this, Jesus went around in Galilee. He did not want to go about in Judea because the Jewish leaders there were looking for a way to kill him. But when the Jewish Festival of Tabernacles was near, Jesus' brothers said to him, "Leave Galilee and go to Judea, so that your disciples there may see the works you do. No one who wants to become a public figure acts in secret. Since you are doing these things, show yourself to the world." For even his own brothers did not believe in him.

Therefore Jesus told them, "My time is not yet here; for you any time will do. The world cannot hate you, but it hates me because I testify that its works are evil. You go to the Festival. I am not going up to this Festival, because my time has not yet fully come." Having said this, he stayed in Galilee.

However, after his brothers had left for the Festival, he went also, not publicly, but in secret. Now at the Festival the Jewish leaders were watching for Jesus and asking, "Where is he?"

Among the crowds there was widespread whispering about him. Some said, "He is a good man."

Others replied, "No, he deceives the people." But no one would say anything publicly about him for fear of the leaders.

John 7:1–13

Day One: Being There

Read slowly through the passage. Remember that in this practice, you are using your imagination to enter the story as a way of spending time with Jesus. Create a short video in your mind, watching the scene unfold. Put yourself into various roles in the scene. Take five or ten minutes to simply imagine the scene, to "daydream" about it. Add details—what smells and sounds surround the action described? What do you see, hear, feel, taste, smell?

Imagine yourself as one of Jesus's brothers. What motivates you to say what you say? How does it feel to argue with your brother, who claims to be the Son of God but doesn't seem to act very messianic?

Imagine you are John, the writer of this passage, watching Jesus interact with his family. What do you notice about Jesus? What is he like? What surprises you about his behavior and words? Does any of it make you uncomfortable? What questions arise?

Spend some time just noticing what is going on, both in the story and in your heart as you imagine yourself in it.

Day Two: Breath Prayer

At the end of this passage, we hear what people are saying about Jesus. He confounded not only his family but other people as well. Who is Jesus to you? Is he a teacher and good example? Is he a confusing person who doesn't do or say what you expect? What one word describes how you are feeling about Jesus these days? Has he been reliable, or does it seem that he's abandoned you? Be still for a few minutes—is there a word that describes your relationship with Jesus right now? Be honest, and not only about how you feel. If Jesus seems "distant," is that something

177

you believe is true of him, or is that because you've been too busy to wait for him?

We sometimes want to fully understand God, but we can't. He's bigger than we're capable of comprehending fully. That's not necessarily a bad thing. We don't always understand or know what Jesus will do; he's unpredictable. Perhaps for you the word to focus on is "mysterious," or "unsearchable," or "holy." God says he's holy, and that doesn't mean religious or pious. It means "set apart"—someone who is other, different, special.

Choose a word that describes Jesus for you right now. Use this word as a prayer. Be still, and when your mind wanders, use this word to bring yourself back to focusing on Jesus. Use your prayer to simply spend time in his presence, to do some deep soul breathing. After your time with Jesus, write the word on your life card.

Day Three: Kindness

Kindness is about putting others first. It is closely related to the discipline of secrecy. Secrecy is not boasting about your spiritual practices or your good deeds. It's simply living the way Jesus told us to in Matthew 6: When you give, don't announce it; when you pray, go in your room and close the door; when you fast, don't make it obvious by your appearance. "Your Father, who sees what is done in secret, will reward you" (Matt. 6:18 NIV). Secrecy is essential to our growth. It is the antidote for "approval addiction," a disease rampant in our society and, truth be told, rampant in me. If we are trying to live the way Jesus did, if we want to breathe deeply, we can't spend all our time talking about our spiritual resumes.

John Ortberg writes: "Vast amounts of human behavior, though painstakingly disguised, are simply attempts at showing off. We want to impress other people without letting on that we're trying to impress them. Approval addiction is the full-blown disease of which showing off may be just one minor symptom."[1]

What was Jesus's motive for secrecy? It seems his brothers wanted him to "show off" a bit. Was he simply afraid of being killed? Or was he listening to God?

Today, practice the discipline of secrecy. Spend some time with God, but don't mention to anyone what you learned or thought about. Do something kind and helpful for someone, but don't mention it to anyone.

Sabbath Reflection

Read the text out loud. Then read slowly through this reflection. It's up to you whether to include your family or others in this practice. If you do include children, depending on their ages, you can read this to them, summarize it, or simply ask them for their observations about the story. If you have a children's Bible, you could read the story from that version. Be open to the idea that they may have some insights that God can use to speak to you. You can use the questions at the end with others or on your own. Use as many or as few of the questions as you like.

"Even his own brothers did not believe in him" (v. 5). When the people in your own family don't believe the best about you, it hurts. We all want respect and support. Sometimes the people we want it from the most don't give it to us.

Jesus was perfect, without sin. But he lived in a very human family. This part of the incarnation—God becoming man—had to be difficult for Jesus. He left the splendor of heaven and the perfect community of Father, Spirit, and himself to come live on earth. When we think about his suffering, we immediately think of his death on the cross. Yes, that was awful. But first he had to suffer the less physically painful but very difficult assignment of having to live and work with human beings. His disciples were stunningly imperfect. He also had to endure the emotional pain of living in a human family.

I guess I figured Jesus had this perfect family. He had a great mom, I think. No argument there. His brothers also were Mary's sons. But despite having a wonderful parent in the woman God chose to bear his Son, Jesus's brothers don't seem so great. This passage exposes Jesus's earthly family's imperfection. It also encourages me as a mom—despite my best efforts, my children will not be perfect. Mary did her best, but in spite of that, her kids (except for Jesus) were imperfect. Why is that encouraging? Because it means that imperfect children are normal and their choices are not necessarily my fault. I will do my best but not blame myself when they make bad choices.

Isaiah predicted that Jesus would be "despised and rejected by men, a man of sorrows, and familiar with suffering" (Isa. 53:3 NIV). Don't you wonder if John, who would have been familiar with that prophecy, thought of it as he watched Jesus in this situation?

The truth it shows us is not just a fulfillment of prophecy, though. It points to the fact that anything we've suffered, Jesus has been through and understands. That includes having to live in an all-too-human, imperfect family. He knows what it is to be misunderstood and to have people who say they love you try to manipulate you.

Jesus's brothers have some boundary issues. They are trying to tell Jesus how to act and what he has to do. They're offering career advice, but they don't understand his mission. Jesus shows us how to set some healthy parameters.

Sometimes people in your family will offer helpful hints on how you ought to run your life. And maybe you think that to be a good Christian, you ought to take their advice or be nice to them, even though you really know they have no idea what they are talking about. What would Jesus do? He'd smile and be nice, he'd try to make those people happy, right?

Um, in a word, no. Read his response. He essentially tells them, "I confront sin, but you guys don't. You let it slide" (see v. 7). These are not sweet, gentle words. He's not being "nice"—but he's being truthful.

I have a lot to learn from Jesus. Sometimes I try to avoid conflict. When well-meaning friends or family members offer to run my life, I often try to keep the peace by agreeing (even if I have no intention of following their advice). But the popular question "What would Jesus do?" cannot be answered, at least in this instance, by "he would be nice."

Setting boundaries and confronting people who try to distract you from your mission—these are not easy things. But sometimes they're as necessary as breathing.

questions

Do you ever feel like your own family (including extended family and in-laws) doesn't really believe in you? Do people in your life offer you advice that feels manipulative? Do they tell you "you should do this," or "really, I think you ought to do that." How do you respond to those "shoulds" and "oughts"?

In what ways are you like Jesus's brothers? Do you ever find yourself praying in a way that, to be honest, is really telling Jesus what he ought to do? What motivates you to do that? Does it ever seem to work?

Week Twenty-six John 8:1–11

Dropping Our Stones

Jesus went to the Mount of Olives.

At dawn he appeared again in the temple courts, where all the people gathered around him, and he sat down to teach them. The teachers of the law and the Pharisees brought in a woman caught in adultery. They made her stand before the group and said to Jesus, "Teacher, this woman was caught in the act of adultery. In the Law Moses commanded us to stone such women. Now what do you say?" They were using this question as a trap, in order to have a basis for accusing him.

But Jesus bent down and started to write on the ground with his finger. When they kept on questioning him, he straightened up and said to them, "Let any one of you who is without sin be the first to throw a stone at her." Again he stooped down and wrote on the ground.

At this, those who heard began to go away one at a time, the older ones first, until only Jesus was left, with the woman still standing there. Jesus straightened up and asked her, "Woman, where are they? Has no one condemned you?"

"No one, sir," she said.

"Then neither do I condemn you," Jesus declared. "Go now and leave your life of sin."

John 8:1–11

Day One: Deep Listening

Remember, this practice is a kind of listening prayer. As you engage in it, you echo the words of Samuel as a boy: "Speak, for your servant is listening" (1 Sam. 3:10). Pay attention to what God may say, even through a seemingly inconsequential part of the text.

Ask God to speak to you through his Word. Trust that he will. Remember that he knows everything about you and your circumstances and wants to guide you.

Read through the text slowly, out loud if possible. Let the words wash over you. Listen for the word or phrase that jumps off the page at you. Underline it if you like. You may want to say the word out loud.

Read the text a second time, listening for a word or phrase that stands out. Pray as you read, asking God to meet you in the text, to show you what he wants you to know or to be. Write the phrase in your journal or in the margins of this book, and spend a few moments pondering it, repeating the words, listening for what God wants to tell you in those words.

As you read through the text one last time, be aware that Jesus wants to connect with you because he loves you. Just spending time with you delights him. But he also wants to guide you. Be open to how he might want to direct your steps through his unique word to you in this passage.

You may want to write the word and any insights that come to you on your life card. During the rest of the week, look at your word and experience his loving presence all over again.

Day Two: Solitude

When it's hard to get time alone, we often wonder whether the effort to do so is worthwhile. To intentionally spend time alone feels odd, countercultural. Today, read through the passage slowly.

Notice that the woman who is accused of adultery is brought to Jesus by a mob, but she's alone. Adultery, by definition, involves two people. But her partner is not there. Or perhaps there never was a partner and she's being unjustly accused. Women in those days had no rights. To argue with a mob that wanted to stone you might be counterproductive.

In either case, she's alone. And probably feeling scared and lonely. After Jesus makes his poignant statement, "Let any one of you who is without sin be the first to throw a stone at her" (v. 7), the woman is again alone—her accusers disappear. But this time, she's alone with Jesus. She might still be scared. But then she has a life-changing conversation with Jesus.

Why should we spend time in solitude by choice? I think time alone strengthens us. Spending time alone makes solitude begin to feel more normal. We realize that if we are alone, we can survive it and even come to enjoy it. Then when we are alone, whether or not we choose it, we don't need to be afraid, because we know that solitude is not so awful.

As you spend time alone today, remind yourself that like the woman in this story, once you've experienced Jesus's grace, you're never really alone.

Note: You may want to combine your journaling time with your solitude time this week and write out some of your thoughts on being alone.

Day Three: Journaling

Consider and journal about these questions: Have you ever felt like someone else did something wrong and they ought to be punished for it? Has focusing on someone else's sin blinded you to your own? Have you ever complained to God about someone else and the bad things they've done? Read through the passage. What does Jesus say to those who accuse? What is he saying to you?

Sabbath Reflection

Read the text out loud. Then read slowly through this reflection. It's up to you whether to include your family or others in this practice. If you do include children, depending on their ages, you can read this to them, summarize it, or simply ask them for their observations about the story. If you have a children's Bible, you could read the story from that version. Be open to the idea that they may have some insights that God can use to speak to you. You can use the questions at the end with others or on your own. Use as many or as few of the questions as you like.

The Pharisees often came to Jesus trying to figure out who he was and what he was teaching. Their questions consistently seemed to thinly veil a desire to put a label on Jesus. Was he liberal or conservative? Did he really understand the Torah, or was he preaching some new heresy? Often they'd phrase their questions, "Moses said this, but what do you say?" Moses was the writer of their most sacred text, the Torah. The question implies that Jesus's teaching contradicts what they hold most dear.

I think by this point they're asking "What do *you* say?" though they are not very interested in hearing his answer. They've already decided he's a radical who needs to be dealt with. They didn't like what he taught, but I think they also didn't like the attention Jesus was receiving. John notes "all the people gathered around him" and Jesus begins to teach.

185

The Pharisees seem to feel threatened not only by his theology but by his popularity. So they try again to trap him into doing or saying something they can point to as a reason to get rid of him.

But this time, they don't just try to confound him with hypothetical questions. They've never beaten him that way, so now they take things to the extreme. They drag in a woman accused of adultery. They are willing to kill this woman to prove their point. The religious leaders think they know what Jesus will do—he'll offer this woman scandalous grace. And they're right. What they don't realize is how he'll do it.

It's very interesting that they bring only the woman, not a couple, since as we noted earlier, adultery involves more than one person. I think Jesus knew (because of who he was) what had really happened. That's part of what shapes his response.

The text says that Jesus had just sat down in the temple courts to teach. He's in the middle of teaching. The Pharisees have walked in right in the middle of a sermon, perhaps on forgiveness or love. Their disruption would rattle most people. But not Jesus.

"Moses says we should kill her," they say, grabbing the woman with one hand, holding stones in the other. Imagine the woman, perhaps half naked or wrapped in a bedsheet. She's dragged not to some remote place but to the temple, the center of Jerusalem, where many people hear the loud accusations against her. Shame radiates from her downcast face.

Jesus doesn't answer but simply stoops down and starts drawing with his finger in the dirt of the temple court floor. Is he hiding his anger? Is he trying to decide what to do? Is he frustrated by their cruelty, by their hard-heartedness?

Silence is powerful, yet it infuriates the Pharisees, who do not know how to handle this—a rabbi crouched, slowly swirling his index finger through the dust on the ground, almost as if he's ignoring them. They persist and continue to question him.

The Pharisees are like children, running to Jesus, saying, "I'm telling!" In fact, as a parent, I've found that when my children come to me accusing one another, a moment of silence is often the best response, when I can remember to do it. I take a deep breath, look into their eyes, silently pray for guidance, but say nothing. To listen, to wait, to not rush to judgment often diffuses the situation without words.

Songwriter Michael Card writes, "What Jesus did that morning created a space in time that allowed the angry mob first to cool down, then to hear his word, and finally to think about it, be convicted by it and respond—or not. It made time stand still. It was original. It was unexpected. It was a response to the noise and confusion and busyness all around him, yet it was not in the least tainted by the noise. Instead, Jesus' action created a frame around the silence—the kind of silence in which God speaks to the heart. In short, it was a supreme act of creativity. It was art."[1]

Art, yes. But it was also a picture of mercy. What did that silence say to the woman? I think it said the same thing that Jesus said out loud to her after her accusers had slunk away: "Neither do I condemn you" (v. 11).

Those moments of silence were a turning point in this woman's life. She was dragged to the temple, thinking she was going to die. Instead she came away from an encounter with Jesus with a second chance at life. He literally saved her life, before he even said a word. His skillful handling of the situation changed everything for her because it gave her hope.

Jesus's words to this woman are his words to us—he doesn't condemn us but calls us to live a higher life. To leave our sins behind us and move forward, not out of guilt or shame or trying to get our good deeds to somehow balance out our bad choices. Rather, he says, start from a place of freedom, knowing you are not condemned. Live based on that forgiveness and love.

? questions

Think of a time you felt condemned or accused—either by others or by your own conscience. How did you imagine God viewed you in that situation?

What surprises you about Jesus's response to the crowd?

Jesus says two things to this woman, and to us. The first is one we love to hear—he does not condemn us. What a relief! But the second is a bit tougher: leave your life of sin. Our response to grace ought to be obedience. Are there habits or patterns of behavior in your life that you need to "leave" in order to fully enjoy grace and forgiveness?

Think of a situation where you have run to God "telling" on someone else. Who do you want to throw stones at? How does focusing on someone else's shortcomings or mistakes blind us to our own sin? Ponder Jesus's statement to the Pharisees; consider how it fits into your own life.

What stone do you need to drop?

Week Twenty-seven John 13:1–17

Serve One Another

It was just before the Passover Festival. Jesus knew that the hour had come for him to leave this world and go to the Father. Having loved his own who were in the world, he loved them to the end.

The evening meal was in progress, and the devil had already prompted Judas, the son of Simon Iscariot, to betray Jesus. Jesus knew that the Father had put all things under his power, and that he had come from God and was returning to God; so he got up from the meal, took off his outer clothing, and wrapped a towel around his waist. After that, he poured water into a basin and began to wash his disciples' feet, drying them with the towel that was wrapped around him.

He came to Simon Peter, who said to him, "Lord, are you going to wash my feet?"

Jesus replied, "You do not realize now what I am doing, but later you will understand."

"No," said Peter, "you shall never wash my feet."

Jesus answered, "Unless I wash you, you have no part with me."

"Then, Lord," Simon Peter replied, "not just my feet but my hands and my head as well!"

Jesus answered, "Those who have had a bath need only to wash their feet; their whole body is clean. And you are clean, though not every one of you." For he knew who was going to betray him, and that was why he said not every one was clean.

*When he had finished washing their feet, he put on his clothes and returned
to his place. "Do you understand what I have done for you?" he asked them.
"You call me 'Teacher' and 'Lord,' and rightly so, for that is what I am.
Now that I, your Lord and Teacher, have washed your feet, you also should
wash one another's feet. I have set you an example that you should do as I
have done for you. Very truly I tell you, servants are not greater than their
master, nor are messengers greater than the one who sent them. Now that
you know these things, you will be blessed if you do them."*

John 13:1–17

Day One: Kindness

Read through the passage. Jesus chooses to serve his disciples
in an almost odd way: He washes their feet. Ordinarily, a servant
boy would have been hired for a few pennies to wash the dust off
people's feet. It was obviously not a glamorous job. But Jesus acted
out of love.

Today, perform an act of kindness that you would consider
"beneath" your normal status. Pray for and then watch for an
opportunity to serve as Jesus would.

Be attentive to God's promptings, even if they seem strange to
you. And don't just think about it, follow through on them.

Write a sentence or two on your life card about what you did,
and how you felt about it.

Day Two: Breath Prayer

First, what strikes you about Jesus as you read this passage?
What quality or personality trait shines through? What name for
Jesus flows out of your observation?

190

Second, what desire stirs in you as you read? What do you need from Jesus?

Take these two ideas and let them form a personal breath prayer. For example, you may want to say, "Humble Savior, cleanse me."

Sit quietly and pray your single-sentence prayer, saying it in the space of a single breath. Spend time just being quiet, paying attention to Jesus, simply being still and knowing he loves you. Breathe deeply and slowly.

If your thoughts wander, use that single sentence to focus. Breathe in as you say his name; exhale as you speak your heart's desire.

Day Three: Being There

Read slowly through the text. Imagine the story unfolding like a movie in your mind. Notice details, and even fill some in: A meal is being served—what smells fill the room? Who is serving it? Jesus pours water into a basin—what does that sound like? He washes your feet—how does the water feel on your tired, hot, dusty feet? It's evening, indoors, in a room lit with candles—what do the room and the table look like?

Imagine you are one of the women who were likely there, serving the meal or even participating in all that was going on. Listen in on Peter's conversation with Jesus. What do you think of it? How do you feel while listening to Jesus, seeing him take on the role of a servant?

What do you learn about Jesus as you watch him, as you listen to him? What would you want to ask him?

Take your time as you daydream about the scene, filling in as many details as you can. After your time of meditation, record an observation or two on your life card.

Sabbath Reflection

Read the text out loud. Then read slowly through this reflection. It's up to you whether to include your family or others in this practice. If you do include children, depending on their ages, you can read this to them, summarize it, or simply ask them for their observations about the story. If you have a children's Bible, you could read the story from that version. Be open to the idea that they may have some insights that God can use to speak to you. You can use the questions at the end with others or on your own. Use as many or as few of the questions as you like.

When I was a kid, I loved to go barefoot outside, running through the backyards of the neighborhood and even on the street. My calloused little feet would turn green from the grass and often had tar stains on them because my friends and I would walk on the road in front of our houses, stepping on the tar that had been softened by the summer heat, feeling the delicious squish.

My mother usually demanded a full bath before bed after a day of running, climbing trees, and sweating. But sometimes, when I ran in for supper, she'd send me to the bathroom with instructions to not only wash my hands before eating but also sit on the edge of the tub and wash the dust and dirt off my feet.

Sometimes she or my father would assist me in this, scrubbing with soap to get the day's grime off. I remember the soft feel of water running from the faucet, the gentle rub on my tired feet, how refreshed I felt once my feet were cleaned.

As a mother, I have also washed my children's feet. It's somehow tender, although it seems like a dirty job. If you were washing a stranger's feet, it might seem nasty. But when you are washing your children's feet, it feels like a very pure expression of love. Foot washing is intimate, kind, and also practical—our feet, especially when we run barefoot, need to be cleaned.

Jesus lived in a hot, dusty area. People wore sandals on their feet and walked everywhere. Their feet got dirty. Typically a servant boy would be hired to wash people's feet—a dirty job no one wanted.

Somehow this detail has been neglected. The other Gospel accounts of the Last Supper don't even mention the foot washing. But they point out that the disciples needed help even figuring out what to do for dinner. They know it's Passover and they are supposed to have a special meal. But they ask Jesus what to do. They need help and direction, which Jesus graciously provides (see Matt. 26:17–19; Mark 14:12–16; and Luke 22:7–13).

John doesn't include those details, but he focuses on Jesus's actions before the meal and their meaning. Jesus did not wash the disciples' feet just because they were dusty. He did not wash their feet just because someone had forgotten to hire a servant to do it.

John tells us in verse 1 why Jesus did what he did: "he now showed them the full extent of his love" (NIV).

As Jesus washes Peter's feet, he is patient with Peter's impetuousness, knowing that despite his declarations of devotion, Peter will deny him. He washes each one's feet, even Judas's—although it's very clear that Jesus knows Judas is going to betray him. Can you imagine being Judas, looking at Jesus as he kneels on the floor in front of you, gently scooping the water over your feet, then carefully toweling them off?

After he has washed their feet, he explains that what he's done is both practical and symbolic. "I have set you an example that you should do as I have done for you," he says (v. 15).

Love, he seems to be saying, is not just about how you feel. It is connected to what you do. To love someone, you serve them. He tells his disciples to wash each other's feet. I know some Christians who take this literally and make foot-washing ceremonies a part of worship. I've participated in this a few times, and it is very meaningful. But Jesus's instructions to his disciples, and to us, are not just literal.

Jesus calls us to put aside whatever status or privilege we could rightfully claim and to instead serve others.

John tells us in verse 3 that Jesus knew that God had given him power and that he would soon be returning to heaven to once again reign with God. John writes that Jesus knew these things, "so he got up from the meal, took off his outer clothing, and wrapped a towel around his waist" (v. 4). How's that? He knew he was all-powerful, *so* he decided to be a servant?

It seems incongruous. But Jesus was showing us how to live. We know that we are his beloved children, that he loves us and cares for us. So? So that doesn't mean we get to act superior. It means we are asked to serve.

If you're a parent, you have to bathe your children. You may wash their little feet after they've played outside. It can be an act of tenderness for those you love.

But do you wash the feet of those who would perhaps betray you or refuse to stand up for you? Those who annoy you or don't love you the way you think they should?

I'm not talking literal foot washing here. But I am talking literal service. How do you serve others? Jesus served from a position of strength. He didn't think of himself as weak and therefore unable to choose anything but service. Rather, he knew his power and chose to use it for good. If we know the power within us as children of God, we can choose to serve. We can serve, as Jesus did, from our strength.

questions

What do you think motivated Jesus to serve his disciples in this way?

Think of a time when someone who didn't have to do it served you in some way. How did that feel?

Have you ever washed someone's feet, figuratively speaking? That is, put aside your own status or privilege to serve someone? What was that experience like? What was difficult about it? What was rewarding about it?

What feelings do you experience as you read this story and reflect on it? What do you sense Jesus is calling you to do?

Week Twenty-eight John 20:1–18

He's Alive!

Early on the first day of the week, while it was still dark, Mary Magdalene went to the tomb and saw that the stone had been removed from the entrance. So she came running to Simon Peter and the other disciple, the one Jesus loved, and said, "They have taken the Lord out of the tomb, and we don't know where they have put him!"

So Peter and the other disciple started for the tomb. Both were running, but the other disciple outran Peter and reached the tomb first. He bent over and looked in at the strips of linen lying there but did not go in. Then Simon Peter came along behind him and went straight into the tomb. He saw the strips of linen lying there, as well as the cloth that had been wrapped around Jesus' head. The cloth was still lying in its place, separate from the linen. Finally the other disciple, who had reached the tomb first, also went inside. He saw and believed. (They still did not understand from Scripture that Jesus had to rise from the dead.) Then the disciples went back to where they were staying.

Now Mary stood outside the tomb crying. As she wept, she bent over to look into the tomb and saw two angels in white, seated where Jesus' body had been, one at the head and the other at the foot.

They asked her, "Woman, why are you crying?"

"They have taken my Lord away," she said, "and I don't know where they have put him." At this, she turned around and saw Jesus standing there, but she did not realize that it was Jesus.

He asked her, "Woman, why are you crying? Who is it you are looking for?"

Thinking he was the gardener, she said, "Sir, if you have carried him away, tell me where you have put him, and I will get him."

Jesus said to her, "Mary."

She turned toward him and cried out in Aramaic, "Rabboni!" (which means "Teacher").

Jesus said, "Do not hold on to me, for I have not yet ascended to the Father. Go instead to my brothers and tell them, 'I am ascending to my Father and your Father, to my God and your God.'"

Mary Magdalene went to the disciples with the news: "I have seen the Lord!" And she told them that he had said these things to her.

John 20:1–18

Day One: Deep Listening

Take a few moments to simply sit. Breathe deeply and slowly, reminding yourself that God's Spirit is as close as the air you breathe.

You may want to sit with your palms up to symbolize your openness, your willingness to listen as God speaks to you through his Word. Trust that he will. Open yourself to his presence, to his love.

Read through the text slowly, out loud if possible. Let the words wash over you. Listen for the word or phrase that jumps off the page at you. Underline it if you like. You may want to say the word out loud.

Because this is a longer passage, you may want to focus on just a portion of it. If one section stirs your heart, linger there. Use that paragraph or two for the second and third readings.

As you read that portion of the text a second time, listen again for a word or phrase that stands out. Pray as you read, asking God what he wants you to know or to be. Write the phrase in your journal or in the margins of this book, and spend a few moments pondering it, repeating the words, and simply listening.

As you read through the text one last time, be aware that Jesus knows your name and wants to connect with you because he loves you.

You may want to write the word and any insights that come to you on your life card. Throughout the rest of the week, look at your word and experience his loving presence all over again.

Day Two: Solitude

Sometimes solitude is a bit frightening. What will happen? What if nothing happens? What if God does not show up?

In this week's passage, Mary goes to the tomb of her leader and friend, the man unlike any other, who treated her with love and respect. She knows he's dead, but she's expecting him to be there. But when she arrives, alone and wanting to pray, to grieve—his body is gone. He's not there!

Soon, though, in the midst of her confusion and sadness, he shows up. This week as you spend some time in solitude, trust that Jesus will show up, just as he did for Mary.

After spending some time in solitude, write a sentence or two on your life card about your experience. If it was disappointing or frustrating, be honest about that. If questions came to mind, write them down. Perhaps like Mary at the beginning of this passage, you are wondering where Jesus is. If Jesus showed up in your time of quietness, make a note of that—so that you have a record of his faithfulness to you.

Day Three: Breath Prayer

What feelings does this story stir in you? What do you want to say to Jesus after reading it? What do you notice about Jesus? What traits stand out in this story?

Reflect on your answers to these questions, and let them form a single-sentence prayer that expresses your name for Jesus and your deep longing. Sit and breathe deeply. When you are quiet, say your prayer on a single in-and-out breath.

Mary recognizes Jesus only after he speaks her name. Her first instinct is to pray, really. The name she calls him, "Rabboni," means "teacher." It expresses her love and respect for him but also her desire: teach me, help me to understand. Clarify for me—what's going on?

Jesus knows your name too. He calls to you and waits for you to respond not only with your love and respect but also with the deepest needs of your soul, which he wants to meet.

Write your one-sentence breath prayer on your life card. Whenever you have a few moments—on a break at work, while folding laundry, or waiting to pick up a child from soccer practice—pull out the card, take a few deep breaths, and pray.

Sabbath Reflection

Read the text out loud. Then read slowly through this reflection. It's up to you whether to include your family or others in this practice. If you do include children, depending on their ages, you can read this to them, summarize it, or simply ask them for their observations about the story. If you have a children's Bible, you could read the story from that version. Be open to the idea that they may have some insights that God can use to speak to you. You can use the questions at the end with others or on your own. Use as many or as few of the questions as you like.

This passage begins, "Early on the first day of the week" (v. 1). Jesus was crucified on a Friday. He was hastily put in a tomb late Friday, before sunset. Why? Because the Sabbath was coming. The last verse of the previous chapter notes that it was "the day of Preparation"—the day before the Sabbath (John 19:42). No one could work on the Sabbath. They could not even tend to Jesus's body.

Imagine Mary, who stood and watched Jesus die on Friday, sobbing with John and the other women as he suffered. She'd watched Nicodemus and Joseph of Arimathea take Jesus's body and lay it in a borrowed tomb.

The parallel passage in Luke 23–24 notes that Mary and the other women saw Jesus put in the tomb on Friday afternoon, then hurried home to prepare spices and perfume before the Sabbath began. They planned to anoint Jesus's body. But the sun set and the Sabbath began. And they could do nothing but wait. "They rested on the Sabbath in obedience to the commandment" (Luke 23:56).

That Sabbath must have been the longest of Mary's life. If she'd ever been tempted to not keep the Sabbath, it certainly would have been on that day. I think I would have wanted, on that day of all days, to *do* something. She would have wanted to be at his grave site. She would have wanted to anoint his body with spices and perfume, as was customary. But she didn't. She obeyed the commandment to rest, although her heart may have been quite restless.

What if Mary hadn't obeyed? Sabbath-keeping is always an act of trust—to believe that the world will keep spinning without us running on the treadmills of our lives. What prayers did she pray?

What if she hadn't obeyed, hadn't trusted? What if she'd run out, unable to wait? Would she have found the tomb still holding Jesus's body?

But she did obey. The Sabbath ended at sunset on Saturday, and the next day Mary was off and running before the sun even rose. Did she even sleep that night? Imagine her hurrying along, carrying spices in a cloak she wears to ward off the early morning chill. She almost jogs along the road to the tomb.

She finds the tomb empty. Empty. She doesn't know what to do. So now she does run—back to Peter and the "other disciple," who in turn sprint to the tomb, then leave, confused and dejected.

But Mary stays. She's exhausted—physically, emotionally, spiritually. She feels, perhaps, abandoned. Her Savior and teacher has died, the other disciples have gone home, Jesus's body isn't even there. She just weeps, overwrought and overwhelmed.

As if that were not confusing enough, she sees two angels in the tomb, and they even speak to her. I wonder if she thought it was all a dream—both terrible and surreal.

And then she sees Jesus, but she doesn't know it is him. All these people—angels, an inquisitive gardener, but no Jesus. Her frustration makes her bold, and she says to the man she thinks is a gardener, "Tell me where he is, and I will get him. I'll pick up his dead body and carry it back home." I can hear her, her voice rising in pitch and tempo. She's a bit irrational, which is not surprising, really. It's because she's tired but also because she loves Jesus.

But then, in a single word, Jesus rewards her obedience and trust. He returns her love with the sweetest thing he could say: her name. "Mary." It's all he says, and it's enough. Immediately she recognizes him. Runs to him, perhaps embraces him, perhaps falls before him, clinging to his feet. She's not shy or distant, we know from Jesus's response: "Don't hold on to me, Mary. Don't stay here. Declare to the others what you've been privileged to be the first to know—that I am risen. I am alive!"

Obeying when it seemed impossible, trusting when it didn't make sense—that's what Mary did. On the other side of that impossible waiting was an amazing gift: the privilege of being the very first person to see Jesus resurrected, the honor of being the one who would bring the amazing news to all the other disciples. She honored him with her obedience, and he honored her.

And he also offered her this: hope and new life. It's what he wants to give each of us, if we are willing to trust.

questions

If you had been Mary, would you have kept the Sabbath that day while Jesus lay in the tomb? What do you think went through her mind?

Describe a time you had to obey by waiting. What was that like?

Have you ever, like Mary, received a blessing from God when you waited and trusted him? Tell about it.

Notes

Introduction

1. For a more detailed explanation of this concept, see Rob Bell, *Velvet Elvis* (Grand Rapids: Zondervan, 2005), 47–49.

2. See Keri Wyatt Kent, *Breathe: Creating Space for God in a Hectic Life* (Grand Rapids: Revell, 2005).

3. For more detail see Marjorie Thompson, *Soul Feast* (Louisville: Westminster John Knox, 1995), 22–25. Her entire week on spiritual reading is highly recommended.

4. Robert Mulholland, *Shaped by the Word: The Power of Scripture in Spiritual Formation* (Nashville: Upper Room Books, 2000), 56–57.

5. MethodX, "Ignatian Method," Upper Room Ministries, 2006, http://www.upperroom.org/methodx/thelife/prayermethods/ignatian.asp.

6. David Benner, *The Gift of Being Yourself* (Downers Grove, IL: InterVarsity, 2004), 37–38. See all of week two of this book for a more detailed explanation.

7. I suggest reading all of the short New Testament book of 1 John—it is all about living out our faith.

Week One: Don't Judge—Ask, Seek, Knock (Matthew 7:1–8)

1. Dallas Willard, *The Spirit of the Disciplines* (New York: Harper & Row, 1988), 28.

Week Two: Jesus's Power to Heal (Matthew 8:1–13)

1. The New Living Translation or *The Message* paraphrase by Eugene Peterson are both excellent and may provide a fresh perspective on familiar passages.

2. The website http://www.methodx.org has some helpful information on all kinds of spiritual practices, including this one. I recommend taking a look at it.

Week Four: Sending Out Rookies (Matthew 10:1–20)

1. John Ortberg, *If You Want to Walk on Water, You've Got to Get Out of the Boat* (Grand Rapids: Zondervan, 2001), 79.

Week Nine: Two Daughters (Mark 5:21–43)

1. Catherine Clark Kroeger and Mary J. Evans, eds., *The IVP Women's Bible Commentary* (Downers Grove, IL: InterVarsity, 2002), 554.

2. Kent, *Breathe*, 153.

Week Twelve: The Greatest Command (Mark 12:28–34)

1. The Holy Bible, King James Version (Cleveland: World Publishing, 1969), Bible Dictionary s.v. "scribe."

Week Sixteen: A Son, and Hope, Resurrected (Luke 7:11–17)

1. Catherine Clark Kroeger and Mary J. Evans, eds., *The IVP Women's Bible Commentary* (Downers Grove, IL: InterVarsity, 2002), 569.

Week Seventeen: Who Loves Much? (Luke 7:36–50)

1. See Frank Gaebelein and J. D. Douglas, eds., *The Expositor's Bible Commentary* (Grand Rapids: Zondervan, 1984), 8:903.

2. For a great explanation of the customs of Jesus's time, see James M. Boice, *The Parables of Jesus* (Chicago: Moody, 1983), 170.

Week Nineteen: A Woman Set Free (Luke 13:10–17)

1. Kroeger and Evans, eds., *The IVP Women's Bible Commentary*, 577.

Week Twenty-two: Bridging the Divide (John 4:1–26)

1. Donald Miller, *Searching for God Knows What* (Nashville: Thomas Nelson, 2004), 133–34.

Week Twenty-three: Take Him at His Word (John 4:43–54)

1. There's some dispute among scholars as to Cana's location, but I'm basing my distance estimate on a map on www.bible-history.com/maps (lower galilee) that shows the distance as being a little more than twenty-five miles away—a long hike. This father risked a fifty-mile round trip hoping Jesus could heal his son.

Week Twenty-five: Unbelieving Brothers (John 7:1–13)

1. John Ortberg, *The Life You've Always Wanted* (Grand Rapids: Zondervan, 1997), 160.

Week Twenty-six: Dropping Our Stones (John 8:1–11)

1. Michael Card, *Scribbling in the Sand* (Downers Grove, IL: InterVarsity, 2002), 16.

About MOPS

You take care of your children, Mom. Who takes care of you? MOPS® International (Mothers of Preschoolers) provides mothers of preschoolers with the nurture and resources they need to be the best moms they can be.

MOPS is dedicated to the message that "mothering matters" and that moms of young children need encouragement during these critical and formative years. Chartered groups meet in approximately four thousand churches and Christian ministries throughout the United States and in thirty other countries. Each MOPS program helps mothers find friendship and acceptance, provides opportunities for women to develop and practice leadership skills in the group, and promotes spiritual growth. MOPS groups are chartered ministries of local churches and meet at a variety of times and locations: daytime, evenings, and on weekends; in churches, homes, and workplaces.

The MOPPETS program offers a loving, learning experience for children while their moms attend MOPS. Other MOPS resources include *MOMSense®* magazine and radio, the MOPS International website, and books and resources available through the MOPShop.

There are 14.3 million mothers of preschoolers in the United States alone, and many moms can't attend a local MOPS group.

These moms still need the support that MOPS International can offer! For a small registration fee, any mother of preschoolers can join the MOPS♥to♥Mom Connection® and receive *MOMSense* magazine six times a year, a weekly Mom-E-Mail message of encouragement, and other valuable benefits.

Find out how MOPS International can help you become part of the MOPS♥to♥Mom Connection and/or join or start a MOPS group. Visit our website at www.MOPS.org. Phone us at 303-733-5353. Or email Info@MOPS.org. To learn how to start a MOPS group, call 1-888-910-MOPS.

Keri Wyatt Kent is a freelance writer, popular retreat speaker, and the author of several books, including *Breathe: Creating Space for God in a Hectic Life,* and *Listen: Finding God in the Story of Your Life.* She lives with her husband and two children in Illinois. To inquire about having Keri speak to your group, sign up for her free newsletter or learn more about her ministry, visit www .keriwyattkent.com.

"Slow down. Find a comfortable chair. Fix a (decaffeinated) beverage and learn how to live one moment at a time."

John Ortberg, pastor and best-selling author of *God Is Closer Than You Think*

breathe

Creating Space for God in a Hectic Life

keri wyatt kent

"Slow down. Find a comfortable chair.
Fix a (decaffeinated) beverage and learn how to live
one moment at a time."

—JOHN ORTBERG,
author, *God Is Closer Than You Think*